Milk Quality

Edited by

F. HARDING
formerly Technical Director
Milk Marketing Board
Thames Ditton
Surrey
UK

BLACKIE ACADEMIC & PROFESSIONAL
An Imprint of Chapman & Hall

London · Glasgow · Weinheim · New York · Tokyo · Melbourne · Madras

Published by Blackie Academic and Professional, an imprint of Chapman & Hall
Wester Cleddens Road, Bishopbriggs, Glasgow G64 2NZ

Chapman & Hall, 2–6 Boundary Row, London SE1 8HN, UK

Blackie Academic & Professional, Wester Cleddens Road,
Bishopbriggs, Glasgow G64 2NZ, UK

Chapman & Hall GmbH, Pappelallee 3, 69469 Weinheim, Germany

Chapman & Hall USA, 115 Fifth Avenue, Fourth Floor, New York NY
10003, USA

Chapman & Hall Japan, ITP-Japan, Kyowa Building, 3F,
2-2-1 Hirakawacho, Chiyoda-ku, Tokyo 102, Japan

DA Book (Aust.) Pty Ltd, 648 Whitehorse Road, Mitcham 3132, Victoria,
Australia

Chapman & Hall India, R. Seshadri, 32 Second Main Road, CIT East,
Madras 600 035, India

First edition 1995

© 1995 Chapman & Hall

Typeset in 10/12pt Times by Acorn Bookwork, Salisbury, Wiltshire
Printed in Great Britain by St Edmundsbury Press, Bury St Edmunds,
Suffolk

ISBN 0 7514 0354 7

A catalogue record for this book is available from the British Library

Library of Congress Catalog Card Number: 95-76793

∞ Printed on acid-free text paper, manufactured in accordance with
ANSI/NISO Z39.48-1992 (Permanence of Paper)

Preface

Milk has played a major contribution to the human diet in many different countries across the world since the dawn of time.

The dairy cow was domesticated over 6000 years ago, she was the object of worship in the Middle East 2000 years before Christ, and milk and milk products are mentioned more than 50 times in the Bible. Milk and dairy products have become a major part of the human diet in many countries. It is not surprising therefore, that over many years considerable attention has been paid to improving the quality of milk. We have worked to improve the yield, the compositional quality and the hygienic quality, and have striven to minimise the level of contaminants which can find access to this, perhaps our most natural, unrefined and highly nutritious foodstuff.

The chain of people involved in the milk industry extends from milk production—farmers, veterinarians and farm advisors—through transport to processing—quality controllers, manufacturers—and on to retailers, legislators, nutritionists, dairy educators and consumers.

All will be interested in the quality parameters of milk which are regularly measured for commercial reasons, for trade, for legal requirements and for reasons of nutrition.

This book aims to provide easily understood background knowledge of milk quality problems, and to give help and solutions to those committed to improving milk quality. The book identifies the quality parameters of significance, explains what they are, why they are important and why they are measured—the principle of measurement and how and where milk is sampled and tested. Most important of all, the value of good quality milk and how it can be produced and maintained are stressed.

The book is therefore intended as a comprehensive source of information and guidance to all involved through the chain of production, processing and handling of milk from cow to consumer.

Acknowledgement

I am grateful to my son Jonathan whose self-taught computer skills not only amaze a computerphobe like me but have been absolutely invaluable in the production of this book.

F. Harding

Note

Analytical methods for milk have been standardised by a number of National and International Standardisation Organisations, from whom detailed published procedures can be obtained. Several sampling and analytical methods are specifically referenced in the text and are obtainable from the appropriate organisation. These Standardisation Organisations are:

ISO   International Standards Organisation
PO Box 250
3830 Ag Leusden
The Netherlands

IDF   International Dairy Federation
Square Vergote 41
1040 Brussels
Belgium

BSI   British Standards Institute
Linford Wood
Milton Keynes
MK14 4BLE
England

Contributors

Frank Harding   Formerly Technical Director, Milk Marketing
Board of England and Wales, Thames Ditton,
Surrey, UK

Robert Harmon   University of Kentucky, College of Agriculture,
Animal Sciences, 414 W.P. Garrigus Building,
Lexington, Kentucky, 40546–0215, USA

Walther Heeschen   Bundesanstalt für Milchforschung,
Institut für Hygiene, Hermann-Weigmann-Str. 1,
24103 Kiel, D-24121, Germany.

Stephen C. Nickerson   Louisiana State University Agricultural Center,
Louisiana Agricultural Experimental Station,
Hill Farm Research Station, Route 1, Box 10,
Homer, Louisiana 71040–9604, USA

Contents

11 Nutritional aspects   **151**
F. HARDING

Index   **163**

1 World milk production

F. HARDING

In 1970 there were 3.6 billion people on the earth; by 1992 the population was 5.4 billion and by the year 2030 it is estimated that it will be 10 billion. Such an explosion of the world's population demands an increase in the world food supply. The world food production rate has increased at a rate of 2.3% per year which is in excess of the population growth of 1.8%.

Against such a background one would have expected the world cow population and the number of dairy farms to be increasing year by year. However, the opposite is the case. The dairy cow population worldwide is about 280 million, but numbers decline year upon year by about 0.3%. The change in cow population varies around the world with the greatest decrease being in the EU which showed a decrease of about 6%. Canada and the USA showed a decrease of about 3% whereas increases were recorded in developing countries.

Part of the reason for these surprising statistics is seen in Table 1.1 which shows that dairy farmers are to a large extent victims of their own success in that the yield of milk per cow has increased significantly over the years. Table 1.1 also shows that the number of cows per farm is increasing as farming in most countries is becoming a business rather than a small family unit. These changes in farming practices have led to over-production in many developed countries resulting in the removal of support mechanisms and, in EU countries and Canada, the introduction of quotas which have limited production.

The 280 million dairy cows in the world produce over 400 million tonnes of milk worth an estimated US$110 million per year. Cow's milk represents about 90.8% of the world milk production with buffalo, sheep and goats producing 6%, 1.7% and 1.5% respectively. Consumption statistics show that about 94% of the world milk supply is utilised as processed milk or milk products (Table 1.2).

Statistics show that the percentage of the world production of milk consumed as liquid milk has fallen from 49% in 1953 to 27%, with cheese consumption showing an increase from 13% in 1955 to 33% at the time of writing.

The full retail value of milk and milk products will only be realised if quality is maximised. It is therefore in the best commercial interests of everyone in the chain, from production, through transport processing and

Table 1.1 Changes in milk production within the EU[a]

	1980	1990	2000 (estimated)
Number of cows/farm ($\times 10^3$)	14.3	19.5	25/30
Number of farms ($\times 10^3$)	1740	1080	450/500
Yield per cow (kg)	4222	4606	5300

[a]Source: *The World Dairy Situation*. IDF, September, 1988.

Table 1.2 World utilisation of cow's milk (1987)[a]

	Tonnes ($\times 10^3$)
Liquid milk	123 134.6
Butter	6900.5
Skim-milk powder	3998.0
Cheese	12 223.8
Whole milk powder	2231.2
Condensed milk	2923.1
Total milk delivered to dairies	387 400

[a]Source: *The World Dairy Situation*. IDF, September 1988.

retailing, to be aware of and to be able to avoid the many pitfalls which can lead to poor quality and diminish the value of milk and milk products.

2 Milk production: Factors affecting milk composition

S.C. NICKERSON

2.1 Introduction

Through genetic selection, improvements in nutrition and management, and advances in milking technology, the mammary gland of the dairy cow yields far more milk nutrients and volume than the calf can consume. Selection of cows for greater production, and the stresses associated with nutrition, reproduction, and the environment may affect milk yield as well as composition. The quantity and quality of milk are highly dependent upon the amount of mammary tissue available to produce milk, secretory cell efficiency in synthesizing milk components, and the availability of suitable nutrients from which the cow manufactures milk. The purpose of this chapter is to provide a basic knowledge of the factors that affect milk yield and composition, which should aid in the development of procedures to efficiently harvest large volumes of a high-quality product. Before such factors can be considered, a basic understanding of mammary gland anatomy, milk storage, and the physiology of milk component biosynthesis and let-down is presented.

2.2 Synthetic and secretory tissues of the mammary gland

2.2.1 Functional anatomy

Each of the four mammary quarters within the udder functions as a separate gland and has its own milk-producing tissues. The spongy tissue (parenchyma) that secretes milk is composed of millions of small globe-like structures (alveoli), which are drained by ducts or tubes into collecting spaces or cisterns (Figure 2.1). The interior of each alveolus is lined by a single layer of secretory epithelial cells. Milk component precursors are absorbed from blood capillaries adjacent to alveoli by these epithelial cells and are converted into milk protein, lactose, butterfat, and other constituents that are released into the lumen or interior of the alveolus for storage between milkings.

As milk accumulates within alveoli, pressure on the epithelial lining causes the secretory cells to become flattened (Figure 2.2a). This signals

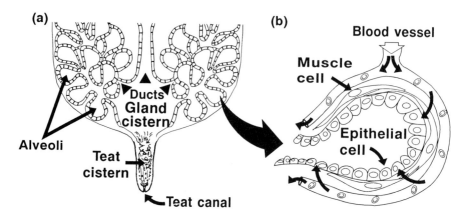

Figure 2.1 (a) Longitudinal diagram of one udder quarter illustrating the milk-producing alveoli (not drawn to scale) and milk-containing spaces. (b) Further enlargement of an alveolus surrounded by muscle or myoepithelial cells, which squeeze milk from alveoli, and blood vessel capillaries, which supply milk precursors to the epithelial cells of the alveolus.

the cells to stop synthesizing milk and releasing it into the lumen. In addition, the surrounding capillaries collapse and the supply of milk precursors is reduced. Immediately prior to milking, approximately 60% of the milk accumulated since the previous milking is held in the alveoli and small ducts, and 40% is stored in the cisterns and large ducts. A network of smooth muscle cells known as myoepithelial cells immediately surrounds each alveolus, and the contraction of these muscle cells leads to the release of milk from the alveoli through the secretory ducts (Figure 2.2b).

2.2.2 Role of the milk-producing cell

The alveolar epithelial cells contain the machinery or organelles necessary to convert precursors absorbed from the blood into milk constituents. An illustration of a typical milk-producing cell of the lactating bovine mammary gland is shown in Figure 2.3. Milk protein, the majority of which is casein, is composed of amino acids that are taken up by the alveolar cells from the blood. Casein is synthesized inside the tube-like rough endoplasmic reticulum, and from this site casein is transported to the Golgi apparatus where it is concentrated in secretory vesicles for export from the cell. Lactose is synthesized in the Golgi apparatus and is secreted from the cell in the same vesicles that transport casein. Calcium, magnesium, and other ions are also secreted via secretory vesicles originating from the Golgi apparatus. Butterfat is synthesized in areas of the cytoplasm occupied by rough endoplasmic reticulum. During secretion,

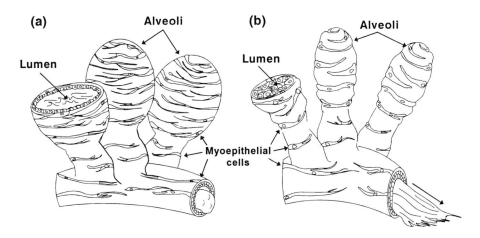

Figure 2.2 (a) Diagram of group of alveoli prior to milking, with one shown in cross-section illustrating accumulation of milk and flattened secretory cells. (b) Alveoli viewed during milk let-down in the contracted state, as milk is forced ventrally to the cisterns.

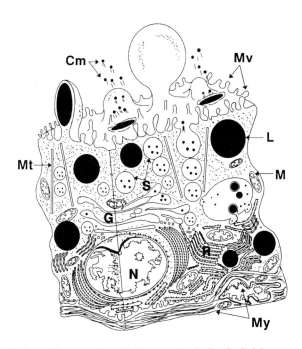

Figure 2.3 Typical milk-producing cell. Cm, casein micelle; G, Golgi apparatus; L, lipid droplet; M, mitochondria; Mt, microtubule; My, myoepithelial cell; Mv, microvilli; N, nucleus; R, rough endoplasmic reticulum; S, secretory vesicle.

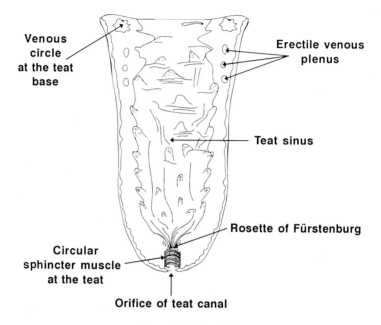

Figure 2.4 The teat.

the droplets push through the cell membrane and are pinched off and released into the alveolar lumen. Microtubules, oriented perpendicular to the apical plasma membrane, guide the flow of secretory products toward the alveolar lumen for release.

2.2.3 *Milk flow within the udder*

The ducts or tubes draining the milk-producing alveolar tissues converge into larger ducts that eventually drain into the collecting spaces or cisterns near the ventral surface of each mammary quarter (see Figure 2.1a). The gland cistern holds 100–2000 ml of milk and empties into the teat cistern below, which holds 10–50 ml of milk. The teat cistern terminates at the teat canal, the opening through which milk is removed (Figure 2.4). The teat canal is 5–13 mm in length and the diameter ranges from 0.40 mm at the distal end to 0.77 mm at the proximal end. With advanced lactation age, the teat canal lengthens and increases in diameter. The teat canal is surrounded by bundles of smooth muscle fibers comprising a sphincter that functions to maintain closure of the canal between milkings. Teats with weak, relaxed, or incompetent sphincters are termed 'patent' or 'leaky'. Cows having such teats milk out in 2–3 min. Cows having teats with tight smooth muscle bundles are called 'hard milkers' because milk is expressed as a fine spray and milk flow is very slow. It may take 10 min or more of milking time to milk-out a hard milker.

2.3 The initiation and establishment of lactation

Under the influence of hormones, the plane of nutrition, and the stimulus of milk removal, milk yield peaks 2–8 weeks after parturition followed by a gradual decline. Persistence of copious milk production depends on maintenance of secretory cell numbers, secretory activity per cell, and efficacy of milk ejection from alveoli. Hormones of the anterior pituitary gland are of paramount importance in the maintenance of lactation. Prolactin is involved in mammary growth and maintenance of lactation, whereas growth hormone stimulates milk production during an established lactation. Secretion of growth hormone appears to increase diversion of nutrients from body stores to the mammary gland, resulting in increased milk yield. Thyroid hormones regulate calcium and phosphorous metabolism. Insulin, produced by the pancreas, is involved in glucose metabolism in the udder, and glucocorticoids from the adrenal cortex are necessary for the initiation and maintenance of lactation. Oxytocin is the hormone essential for milk removal.

2.4 The milk ejection reflex

Between milkings, milk accumulates in the storage spaces of the mammary gland, i.e. the alveoli, ducts, and cisterns. Much of the fluid can be removed from the cisterns and large ducts prior to stimulation of the milk ejection reflex, but milk stored within the alveoli and small ducts cannot be harvested until let-down or the forceful expulsion of milk occurs characterized by a rapid increase in intramammary pressure. This ejection is caused by the contraction of the myoepithelial cells surrounding the alveoli, which indirectly respond to the stimuli associated with milking.

Milking stimuli, such as the touch of a milker's hands and fingers or of wash towels to cows' teats, activate nerve receptors in the skin of the teats. Impulses are carried from these receptors via nerves to the spinal column and up to the brain. Other stimuli, such as the sights and sounds associated with the milking routine, can also initiate the milk ejection reflex and establish a conditioned release of oxytocin. Once a conditional reflex is established, the normal milking routine should be followed, because if the schedule becomes irregular, the conditional reflex will be lost.

When an impulse reaches the brain from the nerve endings of the teat or from visual and auditory sources, oxytocin is released into blood and is

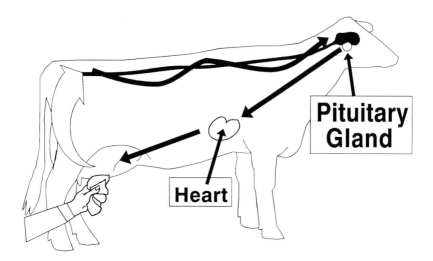

Figure 2.5 Nerves from the udder transmit milking stimuli along the spinal column to the brain and pituitary gland. Let-down hormone (oxytocin) then travels to the udder via the blood.

carried to the mammary gland where it stimulates the contraction of the myoepithelial cells and squeezes milk from the alveoli. The sequence of events is illustrated in Figure 2.5. Teat cups should be attached to the udder 45–60 s after the beginning of udder preparation procedures to allow for maximum intramammary pressure and more complete removal of milk.

Tactile stimulation such as squeezing or massaging of the udder also may elicit some local myoepithelial cell contraction directly without the aid of oxytocin. Thus, massaging a quarter during machine stripping should allow harvest of additional milk from alveoli; however, oxytocin is the primary effector of ejection.

2.5   Effect of breed on milk composition and yield

For the past 15 years, average milk composition has remained fairly constant at 3.6% fat, 3.2% protein, and 4.7% lactose, although production has steadily increased during this period. Butterfat levels have increased in many countries. However, there are factors or conditions under which milk composition is altered. Breed has a profound effect on milk yield but somewhat less of an effect on milk composition. The heavier breeds tend to produce more milk. Holstein/Friesians have the highest mean lactation yield of milk followed by Brown Swiss, Ayrshire, Guernsey, and Jersey.

Table 2.1   Percent milk composition for various breeds of dairy cattle[a]

Breed	Fat	Casein	Whey protein	Lactose	Ash	Total solids
Ayrshire	3.97	2.68	0.60	4.63	0.72	12.69
Brown Swiss	3.80	2.63	0.55	4.80	0.72	12.69
Guernsey	4.58	2.88	0.61	4.78	0.75	13.69
Holstein	3.56	2.49	0.53	4.61	0.73	11.91
Jersey	4.97	3.02	0.63	4.70	0.77	14.15

[a]Source: Adapted from Reinart and Nesbitt (1956).

The percentage of fat tends to be higher in Jerseys and Guernseys, and more variable among individual cows, compared with that of Holstein/Friesians and Ayrshires. Composition also differs, however, among individual animals within a breed. Intrabreed variability is greatest for fat, followed by solids-not-fat (SNF), protein, and lactose.

The effect of breed on milk composition is illustrated in Table 2.1. Significant within-breed differences can be found among a number of studies; however, there is great variability due to geographic location, time of sampling, and herd management factors. For example, the milk of Holstein/Friesians has been found to exhibit fat percentages ranging from 3.62 to 4.54% depending upon the geographic location at which cows were sampled. Temporal differences among studies also exist. For instance, the average percentage fat for the milk of Holsteins in the USA was 3.35% in 1933 but increased to 3.70% in 1960; that for Holstein/Friesians in The Netherlands was 3.10% in 1900 and 4.00% in 1970. Both geographic and temporal variations are most likely a result of genetic selection and progressive changes in management practices. As the composition of the major milk components may vary among breeds, differences also exist among breeds for the composition of some individual components. The protein composition of skim-milk for various breeds is shown in Table 2.2. Similarly, individual components can exhibit genetic variants, especially among Eastern and Western cattle.

2.6   Role of genetics in milk production

Traits of prime economic importance such as milk yield and the percentage of fat are influenced to some extent by genetic factors. The heritabilities of various traits are important because they affect the rate of genetic change of these traits. Heritability is a measure of the degree to which heredity influences a certain trait. The *yields* of milk volume, fat, protein, and total solids have heritabilities of 0.25 (Table 2.3). However, the heritability of milk *composition*, i.e. percentages of fat and protein, is

Table 2.2 Skim-milk protein (g/litre) composition of various breeds[a]

Protein component	Ayrshire	Brown Swiss	Guernsey	Holstein	Jersey
α-Casein	17.1	18.3	19.2	15.8	18.3
β-Casein	8.5	8.4	8.2	6.0	7.6
γ-Casein	0.8	1.1	1.4	2.0	1.3
Immunoglobulin	0.6	0.7	0.8	0.9	0.8
α-Lactoglobulin	1.1	1.1	1.1	1.3	1.5
β-Lactoglobulin	3.1	3.1	3.5	3.0	3.9
Serum albumin	0.3	0.4	0.4	0.4	0.4

[a]Source: Adapted from Rolleri et al. (1956).

Table 2.3 Heritabilities of various traits of dairy cattle important for milk production[a]

Trait	Heritability
Milk yield	0.25
Milk fat yield	0.25
Protein yield	0.25
Total solids yield	0.25
Milk fat (%)	0.50
Protein (%)	0.50
Persistency	0.40
Peak milk yield	0.30
Milking rate	0.40
Mastitis resistance	0.10

[a]Source: Adapted from Wilcox (1992).

higher (0.50). The heritabilities of persistence, peak yield, and milking rate are intermediate, while that for mastitis resistance is quite low. The moderate to high repeatabilities indicate that improvement of these traits would be expected through proper selection procedures.

Daily yield fluctuates somewhat but is highly repeatable (0.95) over a given period (Table 2.4). Repeatability is the tendency of a certain trait to repeat itself in performance over time, i.e. over days or over lactations. The fat content of milk from day to day exhibits greater fluctuation than other components, and has a repeatability of 0.60. Repeatabilities of protein and SNF are higher (more repeatable) at 0.85 and 0.90, respectively. Thus, daily yield and composition would not be expected to change much over a short period of time. Yield is less repeatable from lactation to lactation (0.50) but fat content across lactations (0.75) has a greater repeatability than that found on a daily basis.

A genetic correlation is the tendency for the rate of change of one variable or trait to be associated with that of another variable or trait, and

Table 2.4 Repeatabilities of traits important to milk production[a]

Trait	Repeatabilities	
	Daily	Lactation
Yield	0.95	0.50
Fat (%)	0.60	0.75
Protein (%)	0.85	—
SNF (%)	0.90	—

[a]Source: Adapted from Wilcox (1992).

Table 2.5 Genetic correlations between various milk characteristics and yield[a]

Characteristic	Correlation	Characteristic	Correlation
Fat yield	0.8	Fat (%)	−0.3
Protein yield	0.9	Protein (%)	−0.3
SNF yield	0.9	SNF (%)	−0.2
Total solids yield	0.9	Total solids (%)	−0.3
Chloride (%)	−0.6	Acidity	0.4

[a]Source: Adapted from Wilcox (1992).

varies from −1.00 to +1.00. For example, the yields of fat, protein, SNF, and total solids are highly correlated with milk yield (Table 2.5), whereas percentages of fat, protein, SNF, and total solids are negatively correlated with yield. Chloride is inversely associated with milk yield.

If one trait is selected for, other traits will also change if they are genetically correlated with the selected trait. For example, if one selects for milk yield, it is expected that other milk characteristics will be affected positively or negatively. These changes are illustrated in Table 2.6. Under this selection program, the expected milk yield response per cow per lactation is 273 kg. With selection for milk yield, it is expected that fat yield would increase 10.5 kg, but fat percentage would decrease (−0.036%). Similarly, protein yield would increase but protein percentage would decrease. If fat yield is the trait selected for, then fat yield would be expected to increase 15.6 kg. Concurrently, milk yield would be increased by 199 kg, fat percentage would increase 0.058%, and protein yield as well as percentage would increase. Similar correlated responses can be observed when one selects for protein yield, fat percentage, and protein percentage. Generally, if one selects for milk yield, the yields of other milk solids increase, but their percentages decrease. Alternatively, if one selects to increase the percentage of a given solid, the yield of that solid and the percentage of other solids increase, while milk yield and the yields of the

Table 2.6 Direct (indicated in **bold** type) and correlated responses after a single trait selection[a]

Trait	Milk yield (kg)	Fat yield (kg)	Protein yield (kg)	Fat (%)	Protein (%)
Milk yield	**273**	10.5	6.2	−0.036	−0.18
Fat yield	199	**15.6**	6.3	0.058	0.010
Protein yield	193	10.4	**6.4**	0.014	0.014
Fat (%)	129	10.8	1.5	**0.190**	0.051
Protein (%)	104	3.2	2.7	0.084	**0.075**

[a]Source: Adapted from Wilcox (1992).

other solids change very little. It appears that milk yield is still the best trait on which to base selection.

2.7   Effect of environment on milk composition and yield

Cow's responses to environmental changes are influenced by age, body condition, plane of nutrition, production, and genotoype. For example, young or smaller animals gain and lose heat more rapidly than older, larger animals. Cows that are lactating appear to be more cold resistant but less heat tolerant than nonlactating cows because of the metabolic heat produced by increased feed consumption. *Bos taurus* dairy cows, which are of northern European origin, are more susceptible to stress than *Bos indicus* dairy cows, which evolved in the tropics. It is noteworthy that the latter breed typically exhibits lower basal metabolic rate, lower feed consumption, and as a result, lower milk yield.

2.7.1   Effects of season

Seasonal effects on milk yield and composition are largely attributed to extremes in environmental temperature. The consumption of roughage is reduced during environmental heat stress, resulting in decreased milk production as well as percentage fat. Similarly, milk protein and lactose percentages are lower during the warm season. The differences in milk composition between seasons may average 0.4% fat and 0.2% protein. The milk of cows that calve during the cooler season exhibits greater percentage of fat and SNF than that of cows that calve during the warm season. Under the controlled temperature conditions of one study, temperatures above 29.4°C resulted in increased fat and chloride content, and decreased yield, SNF, protein, and lactose. Between +4.4 and −15°C, percentages of fat, SNF, and protein increased but chloride and lactose contents were not affected. However, in another controlled temperature

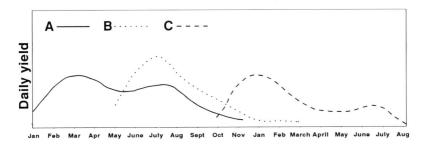

Figure 2.6 Effect of the 'spring flush' on milk production relative to time of calving.
(Source: adapted from Whittemore, (1980).)

study, composition remained unaffected when cows were alternated between 18.3 and 31.1°C.

In some countries, such as the UK, turning cows out onto the lush green pastures of spring raises milk production 10–15%. This phenomenon is known as the 'spring flush' (Figure 2.6). If the spring flush takes place in mid lactation, i.e. cows that calve in Winter (A), the yield for that lactation may increase by up to 500 kg. This is attributed to the effect of maintaining persistency for an extended period of time. For cows that calve in the spring (B), an increase in peak milk yield usually results because of the additive effect of the spring flush, with a subsequent decline in the lactation curve. For cows that calve in the fall (C), milk production has tapered off for that lactation by the time the spring flush is in effect, and the rise in production due to access to spring pasture late in the curve is minimal and brief.

2.7.2 Effects of thermal stress

The stresses associated with hot and cold environmental temperatures adversely affect dairy cattle metabolism by increasing maintenance requirements. Although water intake decreases, feed consumption increases during cold stress, which prevents the decline in milk production until temperatures fall below −5°C. The increase in nutrient uptake is due to increased maintenance requirements, i.e. for metabolic heat production, not increased yield. Alternatively, water intake increases but feed consumption decreases during heat stress, leading to a reduction in milk yield, despite the increase in maintenance requirements. Heat stress decreases consumption by directly affecting feed intake centres in the brain. Likewise, intake is decreased because of increased gut fill due to reduced rate of passage and increased water consumption, and the increased respiration rate to dissipate body heat.

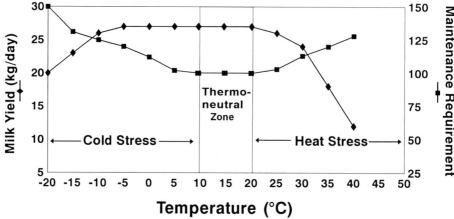

Figure 2.7   Effect of ambient temperature on maintenance requirements and milk yields in cattle. (Source: adapted from McDowell (1981).)

The basal metabolic rate of the dairy cow is fairly constant within the thermoneutral zone. Thus, between 10 and 20°C the animal has the potential to exhibit maximum milk production. However, outside of this zone, heat and cold adversely affect yield. The association of heat and cold stress with yield and maintenance requirements is shown in Figure 2.7.

During the hot summer months, forage consumption is reduced because of its high heat increment, while concentrate consumption is maintained. This reduced intake of forage may alter rumen fermentation, and the acetate:propionate ratio which affects fat production hence may be the cause of reduced milk fat content during periods of environmental heat stress.

Potassium deficiencies may also affect milk yield during heat stress. Increased sweating at these times results in the loss of potassium from dairy cows, thus the dietary requirement for this electrolyte is increased. Feeds low in potassium may not meet the dietary requirement, thus increasing the potassium content of rations low in this element can increase yield in cattle that are chronically exposed to thermal stress.

As observed in Figure 2.7, heat stress causes a more rapid decline in milk production than cold stress. This is because during cold weather, feed consumption is increased to fulfil the animals' maintenance needs. Conversely, during heat stress, feed consumption decreases, despite the increased maintenance requirement, resulting in a more rapid decline in milk production. Heat stress during pregnancy may also adversely affect the endocrine status of the cow, resulting in reduced mammary growth and reduction in subsequent milk production.

Percentages of fat, total solids, and SNF are greatest during the winter months. Most of the seasonal variation in SNF is due to variation in the milk protein content. Percentages of fat and protein are lowest during the summer season and highest during cooler months, in part, due to seasonal changes in forage quality and availability.

It may be beneficial to feed supplemental fat during periods of heat stress. Less heat is generated during the digestion of fat compared with protein and carbohydrate. Thus, feeding supplemental fat during periods of thermal stress may not only reduce the heat load but will also increase the energy density of the diet when feed consumption is reduced. One study showed that feeding supplemental dietary fat during warm weather improved lactation performance but had no effect during cooler months.

Latitude is another environmental factor that affects milk production and composition because of its relationship with the angle of solar radiation and day length. About 50% of the world's cows are located at latitudes between 30°N and 30°S but heat stress also occurs at these latitudes.

2.8 Dairy cattle nutrition and its influence on milk yield and composition

Nutrition is obviously a key factor influencing milk yield and composition, since the milk-producing cells of the mammary gland require a constant and optimum supply of precursors to synthesize milk components. The major substrates absorbed from the blood are glucose, acetate, β-hydroxybutyrate, amino acids, fatty acids, and minerals. The cows' diet can be manipulated to vary the percentages of milk components, some more than others. For example, fat content can be varied over a range of 3.0 percentage units and protein can be varied by 0.6 percentage units but lactose content is not influenced by diet manipulation, except through over-feeding or underfeeding.

2.8.1 Dietary effects on milk fat

Because precursors required by the mammary gland to synthesize fat are generated during fermentation of feedstuffs in the rumen, diets that alter fermentation affect fat content. For example, a low intake ratio of roughage to carbohydrate will result in decreases in acetate and butyrate, which are the major fat precursors, and increases in propionate, which negatively affects milk fat. Studies have shown that on a dry matter basis, the minimum forage to concentrate ratio needed to maintain milk fat content is about 40:60. To maintain the fat content above 3.6%, average forage length should be at least 0.65 cm. Use of forages that are finely ground result in greater propionate production in the rumen, resulting in reduced milk fat.

To maximize fat percentage as well as yield, a minimum of 28% neutral detergent fiber is recommended in the dietary dry matter. Likewise, only the highest quality roughage should be used, because it not only promotes increases in yield, but also results in a high level of acetate production to maintain milk fat content. It should be noted that excess fiber in the ration will reduce dry matter intake, resulting in lowered milk production.

Type of concentrate used in the ration also affects milk fat percentage. Compared with corn-based concentrates, those using barley may reduce the digestibility of fibre. Processing grains used in concentrates by pelleting, grinding, etc. increases the digestion of starch in the rumen and the production of propionate, which subsequently reduces milk fat. Cereal grains as concentrates may be substituted with soluble carbohydrates (lactose, whey, molasses) to alleviate the reduction in percentage fat caused by feeding low-forage rations. These carbohydrates appear to promote the growth of rumen bacteria that produce acetate for fatty acid synthesis.

Fat can be added to the diets of dairy cows in attempts to increase milk fat content. Use of saturated fats in the diet will increase percentage fat somewhat, whereas unsaturated fats decrease fat percentage; however, fat yield usually remains unchanged or increases. Fiber digestion and acetate production can be promoted by incorporating whole or crushed oilseeds into the diet. Processed fats, protected to reduce interaction with rumen microorganisms, can also be used as additives and include fat encapsulated in formaldehyde-treated protein and calcium soaps of fatty acids. Use of protected fats in the ration has been found to increase milk fat content, and additionally, protected fatty acids can alter the fatty acid composition of milk by raising the monounsaturated or polyunsaturated levels.

Other additives also may be included in dairy rations to increase milk fat as well as yield. Corn silage, for instance, if provided as 57% of the diet, will increase both milk yield and percentage fat if sodium bicarbonate is added. Similarly, magnesium oxide will increase yield as well as milk fat content. It is contended that this compound may exert its influence by indirectly improving the transfer of blood lipids to the mammary gland. Inclusion of methionine hydroxy analog in high energy diets has also increased milk fat content and yield.

2.8.2 Influence of ration on milk protein

Amino acids required for milk protein synthesis are derived from microorganisms in the rumen. Thus, the protein content of milk is influenced by factors that regulate microbial growth. In the rumen, the production of propionate promotes milk protein synthesis, possibly by increasing the availability of certain amino acids, such as glutamate. The amount of propionate produced is increased by feeding chopped forage (less than the

0.64 cm recommended to maintain milk fat). Similarly, increases in starch digesting microorganisms promote the production of propionate.

Starch is needed to maintain microbial digestion and subsequent microbial protein synthesis, both of which are positively correlated with milk yield and percentage protein in milk. The source and processing of starch influence fermentation in the rumen, and therefore affect milk composition. For example, the starch in barley and wheat degrades more rapidly than that of corn. If degradation is too slow, microbial digestion and protein synthesis are inhibited, leading to decreased milk yield and percentage protein. Fine grinding of such grains or steam flaking will increase rates of degradation, thereby reducing the depressive effect on yield and protein content.

Rumen microorganisms cannot utilize lipids as an energy source for growth and synthesis of microbial protein. Thus, although added dietary fat provides energy, which may increase yield, percentage milk protein is reduced. It has been recommended that when fat is added to a ration to increase its energy content, then the diet should be enriched with amino acid supplements or undegradable dietary intake protein if the protein percentage of milk is to be maintained. It should be noted that although milk protein percentage decreases when dietary fat is added, the protein yield is unaffected because of the increase in milk production from the energy-enriched ration. If protein is added to rations devoid of supplemental fat, milk protein content is increased slightly, probably through the provision of limiting amino acids. The feeding of protected methionine or corn gluten meal may also increase milk protein percentage.

2.9   The effects of milking management practices on milk quality

2.9.1   Milking interval

During the intermilking period, beginning immediately following the last milking, rate of secretion by alveolar epithelial cells proceeds at a uniform rate until the alveoli expand with milk and exert pressure on the milk-producing cells. This fluid stasis inhibits and eventually stops the synthetic processes. If cows are milked at 10 and 14 h intervals, more milk is obtained after 14 h because of total fluids accumulation; however, the rate of secretion or yield per hour is greater during the 10 h interval. Milking at shorter intervals relieves udder pressure more frequently and allows milk synthesis to continue at an elevated rate, leading to increased daily yield.

Figure 2.8 shows how the accumulation of milk within the udder affects the secretory rate during the intermilking period. Milk synthesis continues at a fairly constant rate through 12 h, then decreases by approximately 50%. During this period, milk pressure is also increasing, which inhibits secretion after 12 h.

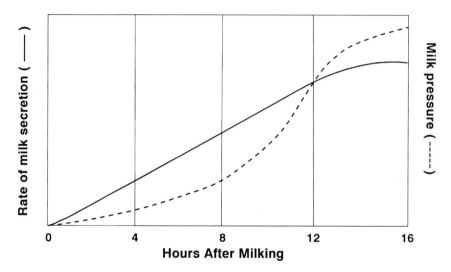

Figure 2.8 Relationship between rate of milk secretion and milk pressure within the udder.

2.9.2 Milking rate

Cows with weak (relaxed) or patent teat sphincter muscles, and wide diameter teat canals may milk out in 3–4 min while those with tighter teat
sphincters and narrow diameter teat canals may take up to 10 min to milk
out. Use of teat canal dilators has generally been unsuccessful due to
leakage of milk and greater risk of intramammary infection. It may be
best to use selective breeding to propagate cows that are fast milkers;
however, such cows may be more prone to mastitis.

The pulsation rate may also affect rate of milk out. High pulsation rates
at low levels of vacuum have a greater effect on increasing milking rate
than at higher vacuum levels. Slow pulsation rates provide insufficient teat
end massage and can lead to pain, which interferes with milk let-down,
daily yield, and the milk fat test. Pulsation ratio also affects milk flow. A
longer milking phase to rest phase ratio may increase milking rate, but
insufficient massage will adversely affect milk ejection, so in the long run,
milking time is extended.

2.9.3 Frequency of milking

If cows are milking more frequently, a greater volume of milk is produced
but the response diminishes with increasing frequency. For instance,
milking twice a day yields 40% more milk than once a day; milking three
times a day yields 5–20% over twice-a-day milking; and milking four

times a day may yield an additional 5–10%. Factors that may contribute to this increased production include less intramammary pressures as a result of frequent milk out, increased stimulation of hormones for milk synthesis, and reduced negative feedback on secretory cells due to the build-up of milk components in alveolar lumena. Only well-managed herds can experience the benefits of milking three times a day over an extended period of time. In the USA the Dairy Herd Improvement Association acknowledges a 15–20% increase in production for cows milked three times a day over those milked twice a day, with the most benefit attributed to younger animals.

2.9.4 Milking routine

Milking routine also influences the quantity and quality of milk. Proper premilking stimuli and timely attachment of teat cups are necessary to take full advantage of oxytocin release and milk let-down for the optimal harvest of milk. In addition, appropriate teat end vacuum must be maintained with a minimum of fluctuation to allow maximum milk flow without leading to teat cup crawl, which can restrict milk flow, or teat and swelling and edema, which can cause pain and interfere with let-down. Such developments lead to reductions in daily yield.

Milking routine can also affect milk composition as well as yield. During the intermilking period, fat droplets, having a lower specific gravity, tend to accumulate in the upper portions of alveoli and remain in the upper regions of larger ducts and cisterns. Therefore, during the milking process, milk fat content continues to increase, and is highest in the strippings fraction. If a cow is not milked out completely, the percentage fat for that milking will be lower, but the fat content will be higher at the next milking because of accumulated fat. Furthermore, when intervals between milkings are unequal, yield is greater but fat percentage is lower after the longer interval because of dilution. When milking intervals are greater than 15 h, rate of secretion is reduced markedly, and concentrations of SNF, lactose, and potassium decrease, but percentages of fat, whey proteins, sodium and chloride increase.

In some studies, milking intervals greater than 16 h led to reduced yield and SNF; percentage fat increased but fat yield decreased because production was reduced. A 15% reduction in production was realised when the milking interval was increased from 8 to 24 h. In low-producing cows, milking interval has less of an effect on daily milk yield compared with high-producing cows. It is generally contended that use of more regular milking intervals has a positive effect on production. For example, in cows milked twice a day, milking every 12 h resulted in a 305 day lactation yield of 6242 kg, whereas using intervals of 16 and 8 h, yield was 6161 kg. Similarly, for cows milked three times a day, those milking at 8 h intervals produced 3.9% more milk and 5.2% more fat than those milked at 6, 7, and 11 h.

2.9.5 Cow preparation and residual milk

Even under excellent milking conditions, some milk is not removed from the udder. This is known as residual milk. The amount of this residual milk varies greatly among cows but may range between 10 and 25% of the total volume present before milking. Residual milk is retained in alveolar lumena and interferes with the capacity to synthesize and secrete new product during the intermilking period. More complete milk removal can be accomplished by increasing the downward and forward tension on the milking unit. This action pulls down on the duct system, providing for better drainage of alveoli and small ducts into cisternal areas for removal.

When cows are disturbed prior to or during the milking process, the amount of residual milk increases. Stray electrical voltage, beating of cows to encourage them to enter the milking parlour, excessive vacuum applied to teat ends, teat sores, etc. can all cause discomfort to the cow and result in incomplete milk removal. Similarly, the volume of residual milk is increased when the milking process does not coincide with the milk let-down process. A delay of 5–10 min in applying teat cups after let-down will reduce intramammary pressure and increase residual milk because the effectiveness of the milk expulsion reflex is transitory and a portion of milk remains in alveoli. For example, when teat cups are attached after a 1 min delay after udder preparation, 11.2% residual milk remains; however, after a 5 min delay, 24.8% residual milk is left (Table 2.7). Consequently, milk yield decreases about 2 kg and fat yield decreases 70 g, although the percentages of bucket milk fat and residual fat actually increase. Thus, large volumes of residual milk result in lower peak flow rates, reduced daily milk production, suboptimal lactation production, and fewer days in milk. A large amount of residual milk also reduces the percentage of fat.

The fact that butterfat rises most likely accounts for the variation in fat content as it leaves the udder. The first-drawn milk may be only 1–2% fat, while at the end of milking, fat percentages between 5 and 10% are not uncommon. Residual milk can contain as much as 20% fat. Changes in milk fat content during milking are explained in Figure 2.9. As the alveoli collapse under the forces of the myoepthelium, milk enters the secretory ducts but some fat remains in the upper alveolar lumen (A) with the residual milk. Variable amounts of fat remain in the lateral alveoli (B). The lower alveoli (C) probably lose much of the fat to secretory ducts before milk ejection occurs. In addition to fat rising, the fat droplets may pass more slowly through alveoli and ducts due to their size and viscosity, thus tend to be moved at a slower rate during the milk ejection process.

Table 2.7 Effect of time delay after udder preparation on milk production characteristics[a]

Production	Delay after preparation	
	1 min	5 min
Residual milk and hand stripping (%)	11.20	24.80
Milk (kg/day)	14.56	12.54
Fat yield (g/day)	563.00	493.00
Fat (%)	3.87	3.93
Residual milk fat (%)	10.10	12.30
Peak flow rate (kg/day)	2.81	2.56

[a]Source: Adapted from Brandsma (1978).

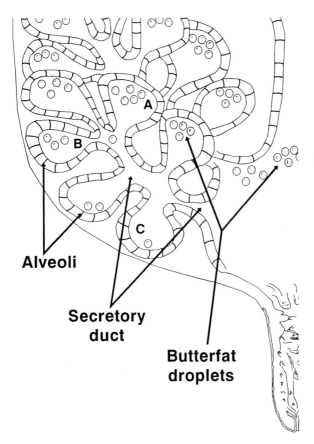

Alveoli

Secretory duct

Butterfat droplets

Figure 2.9 Distribution of butterfat droplets in residual milk of a section of a quarter.

To encourage milk let-down, cows and heifers should be introduced to the milking parlour two or three times a day for several days before calving. A regular routine should be established to optimise the let-down and harvest of milk. For example, the cow should be made comfortable in the milking stall or parlour. Several streams of milk should be stripped from each teat. Teats should be predipped or washed with single-service towels dipped in sanitising solution and dried thoroughly. The time interval from the start of stripping until the end of washing should be at least 25 s. A copious flow of milk should start within 60 s after starting udder preparation, and should peak within 2 min of applying the milking machine. The response is greatly affected by level of milk production, peak milk flow of each cow, diameter of the teat canal, success of milking preparation, and type of milking equipment used.

2.10   Influence of age and stage of lactation on milk component yield

Lactation age, as well as stage of lactation, also influence milk quality. It has been demonstrated that with each successive lactation, the fat content decreases by approximately 0.05 percentage units, and the SNF content decreases about 0.1 percentage units. This is due, in part, to increasing yield up to the fifth lactation and to the increased incidence of mastitis. The peak in yield during the fifth lactation, when the cow is 7–8 years old, also coincides with its maximum skeletal size. During the latter part of each gestation and into the early subsequent lactation, there is new growth and development of milk-producing tissues. Thus, greater production can be expected with succeeding lactations. Milk production maintains a plateau for several years after the fifth lactation, then proceeds to decline beyond 12 years of age. Mammary glands increase in size from the first to the fifth lactation. Because milk production depends on udder size and hormonal stimuli, it is probable that the production pattern in recurring lactations is a reflection of these two phenomena. In general, milk production increases 30% from the first to fifth lactation, but the percentage increase progressively decreases with age. For example, recurring pregnancies and lactations result in increases of approximately 13% in milk production from the first to the second, 9% from second to third, 5% from third to fourth, and 3% from fourth to fifth lactation. A portion of the increase is due to skeleton maturation and an increase in body weight, which can accommodate a larger udder.

Milk composition also changes over lactation. During the immediate postpartum period, colostrum contains much more total protein, casein, whey proteins and minerals but less lactose than the normal milk that appears after several days. The total solids content of colostrum may be as high as 25%. The greatest difference in composition between colostrum

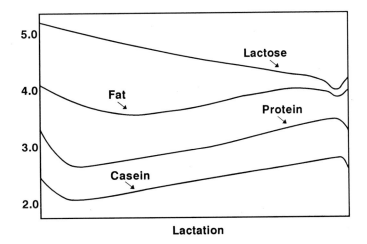

Figure 2.10 Changes in milk solids during lactation. (Source: adapted from Politiek (1957).)

and milk is the elevated content of antibodies in colostrum (up to 10%), which are transferred to the newborn calf. Of the minerals, calcium, sodium, magnesium, phosphorus, and chloride are higher than in milk but potassium content is lower. Figure 2.10 illustrates the changes in milk solids over lactation. These changes in composition that occur during the first few days postpartum, continue for approximately 6–8 weeks but at reduced rates. The total percentage of SNF is elevated at the initiation of lactation but declines steadily until 6–8 weeks postpartum. After this time, the increase in protein counters the decrease in lactose, thus the SNF content tends to remain rather constant through the eighth month. Then SNF content increases due to the circulating hormones of pregnancy. In unbred cows, the percentages of SNF as well as fat exhibit gradual declines over the remainder of the lactation.

References and further reading

Brandsma, S. (1978) The relation between milking residual milk and milk yield. In *Proc. Symp. on Machine Milking 17th Ann. Meeting*. National Mastitis Council, Inc., Arlington, VA, USA, p. 47.

Emmerson, M.A. (1941) Studies on the macroscopic anatomy of the bovine udder and teat. *Vet. Ext. Quart.*, **41**, 80.

Gifford, W. (1936) The butterfat records of cows possessing supernumeraries compared with cows having the normal number of teats. *Mo. Agric. Exper. Sta. Bull*, **370**, 42–47.

Hammond, J. (1927) *The Physiology of Reproduction in the Cow*. Cambridge University Press, Cambridge, UK.

Larson, B.L. (1985) *Lactation*. The Iowa State University Press, Ames, IA, USA.

Larson, B.L. and Smith, V.R. (1974). *Lactation: A Comprehensive Treatise* (Vol. III: Nutrition and Biochemistry of Milk/Maintenance). Academic Press, New York, USA.

Linzell, J.L. (1955) Some observations on the contractile tissue of the mammary glands. *J. Physiol*, **130**, 257–267.

McDowell, R. (1981) *Effect of Environment on Nutrient Requirements of Domestic Animals* (79). National Research Council, National Academy Press, Washington, DC, USA.

Mein, G.A., Clough, P.A., Westgarth, D.R. and Thiel, C.C. (1970) A comparison of the milking characteristics of transparent and conventional teatcup liners. *J. Dairy Res.*, **37**, 535–548.

Murphy, J.M. (1959). The effect of certain mild stresses on the bovine teat canal on infection with *Streptococcus agalactiae*. *Cornell Vet.*, **49**, 411–421.

Noorlander, D.O. (1960) *Milking Machines and Mastitis*. Californian Compton Press, CA, USA.

Reitsma, S.Y., Cant, E.J., Grindal, R.J., Westgarth, D.R. and Bramley, A.J. (1981) Effect of duration of teatcup liner closure per pulsation cycle on bovine mastitis. *J. Dairy Sci.*, **64**, 2240–2245.

Rolleri, G.D., Larson, B.L. and Touchberry, R.W. (1956) Protein production in the bovine breed and individual variations in the specific protein constituents of milk. *J. Dairy Sci.*, **39**, 1683.

Smith, V.R. (1964) Anatomy of the udder. In *Physiology of Lactation*. The Iowa State University Press, Ames, IA, USA, pp. 16–49.

Swett, W.W. (1942) Arrangement of the tissues by which the cow's udder is suspended. *J. Agric. Res.*, **65**, 19–22.

Turner, S.W. (1981) *Harvesting your Milk Crop*. Babson Bros., Dairy Research and Educational Service, Oak Brooks, IL, USA.

Van Horn, H.H. and Wilcox, C.J. (1992) *Large Dairy Herd Management*. ADSA, Champaign, IL, USA.

Whittemore, C.T. (1980) *Lactation of the Dairy Cow*. Longman Group Ltd, New York, USA.

Wilcox, C.J. (1992) *Genetics: Basic concept. Large Dairy Herd Management* (eds Van Horn, H.H. and Wilcox, C.J.). ADSA, Champaign, IL, USA, pp. 1–8.

Williams, D.M., Mein, G.A. and Brown, M.R. (1981) Biological responses of the bovine teat to milking: Information from measurements of milk flow rate within individual pulsation cycles. *J. Dairy Res.*, **48**, 7–21.

3 Mastitis and milk quality

R. HARMON

3.1 Introduction

Mastitis is defined as an inflammation of the mammary gland. The inflammation is a response of the tissue to injury. The purposes of the inflammatory response are to destroy or neutralize the injurious agent and allow healing and return to normal function. A key component of inflammation is the influx of white blood cells or leukocytes which results in an increase in the somatic (body) cell count (SCC) of milk. Thus, the SCC is a common measure of mammary gland health and milk quality. Although inflammation can result from a variety of types of injury including infectious agents, physical trauma, or chemical irritants, mastitis in dairy cattle is generally the result of microorganisms which enter the mammary gland, multiply and produce toxins that cause injury to the mammary tissue. It is believed that mediators of inflammation may contribute to some of the pathophysiological responses in severe cases of mastitis. Bacteria are the most common causes of mastitis, but other types of organisms such as yeasts, mycoplasmas, and algae may occasionally infect the udder.

Mastitis is considered the most costly disease complex in the dairy industry resulting in decreases in milk production, increased production costs, and reduced milk quality, despite advances made in mastitis control over the past 20–30 years. The widespread occurrence of the disease in dairy herds creates an estimated loss to producers of approximately US $2 billion in the US alone. This excludes the additional untold losses that occur once milk has left the farm due to altered milk quality and composition and the effects on dairy products. This discussion will focus primarily on bovine mastitis, because of the impact of this disease on the dairy industry from the dairy farm to the consumable product.

3.2 Causative organisms

The causative bacteria can be categorized as major or minor pathogens. The most common major pathogens include *Staphylococcus aureus, Streptococcus agalactiae*, the coliforms, and streptococci and enterococci of environmental origin. Individual cases or sporadic outbreaks of mastitis may be caused by *Pseudomonas* spp., *Actinomyces pyogenes*, *Serratia* spp., or other unusual pathogens. Mastitis caused by the major pathogens results in the greatest compositional changes and increases in somatic cell count in milk and has the most economic impact. Coagulase-negative staphylococci and *Corynebacterium bovis* are considered minor pathogens. Infections by these organisms cause only moderate inflammation with somatic cell counts exceeding those of uninfected glands by only two- to three-fold. Minor pathogen infections are rarely associated with clinical mastitis, compositional changes, or dramatic decreases in milk production.

3.3 Contagious and environmental pathogens

Staphylococcus aureus and *Streptococcus agalactiae* are contagious mastitis pathogens. The major reservoir for these pathogens is the infected udder, and infections are spread from cow to cow during the milking process. Infections tend to be chronic and subclinical with periodic clinical episodes. The environmental pathogens include the coliforms and environmental streptococci and enterococci. The coliforms are a group of Gram-negative pathogens that include *Escherichia coli*, *Klebsiella* spp., *Enterobacter* spp., and *Citrobacter* spp. *Streptococcus dysgalactiae*, *Streptococcus uberis*, *Streptococcus bovis*, *Enterococcus faecium*, and *Enterococcus faecalis* are common environmental streptococci and enterococci. As the term would suggest, the source of environmental pathogens is the surroundings of the cow, e.g. bedding, manure, and soil. Although new infections by environmental pathogens may occur at milking time, primary exposure appears to be between milkings. Approximately 70–80% of coliform infections will become clinical (abnormal milk, udder swelling, or systemic symptoms), and about 50% of environmental streptococcal infections display clinical symptoms. Sixty to 70% of environmental pathogen infections will exist for less than 30 days.

3.4 Inflammation

Infections of the mammary gland by pathogenic bacteria result in decreases in milk production and compositional changes that vary with the intensity and duration of the infection. Subclinical infections are those with no visible changes in the appearance of the milk or the udder, but milk production decreases, bacteria are present in the secretion, and composition is altered. Clinical mastitis is characterized by abnormal milk, swelling or pain of the udder, and may be accompanied by systemic signs such as elevated rectal temperature, lethargy, or anorexia. As in subclinical mastitis, milk production declines, bacteria are present in the milk, and dramatic changes in milk composition are usually present.

An inflammatory response is initiated when bacteria enter the mammary gland through the teat canal, multiply in the milk, and produce toxins. One of the initial components of the inflammatory response that is a major line of defense for the udder is the influx of white blood cells or poly-morphonuclear neutrophil (PMN) leukocytes into the mammary tissue (Figure 3.1). The PMN normally flow freely through capillaries with only minimal sticking to vessel walls. During infection and inflammation PMN marginate or stick to the wall of smaller blood vessels and pass between cells lining the vessel. Chemical messengers or chemotactic agents released from leukocytes normally in the milk or from damaged tissues attract PMN into milk in large numbers. The PMN appear in large numbers lined up outside some alveoli. In other areas damage to milk-synthesizing cells may be apparent with masses of PMN passing between epithelial cells into the lumen of the alveolus. Thus, the end result of this process is an increase in the SCC in milk resulting from PMN migration to the site of infection. Figure 3.2 shows an electron micrograph of mammary tissue from an infected udder demonstrating the migration of PMN across the mammary epithelium in an end-to-end fashion. PMN can also be observed migrating through the linings of teat and duct cisterns. These areas may be sites of migration during the initial response to invasion.

The function of PMN in milk is to engulf and digest the invading bac-teria. When PMN enter milk they also engulf other particles such as fat globules and casein, which decreases their efficiency compared with that of blood cells (Figure 3.3). However, PMN still remain a key defense mechanism in the udder. The leukocytes in milk may also release specific substances which change the permeability of blood vessels or attract more leukocytes to the area to fight the infection. In persistent bacterial infec-tions, leukocyte numbers may fluctuate up and down, but will generally remain abnormally high. Such abnormal numbers of somatic cells will continue after bacteria are eliminated until healing of the gland occurs.

In addition to elevated somatic cell numbers, infection causes a number of other events in the mammary gland. Toxins produced by bacteria damage milk-producing tissue, resulting in less total synthesis of milk (Figure 3.4). Changes in the permeability of blood vessels and mammary epithelium lead to the leakage of blood components into milk and the movement of some normal milk components out of the alveolar lumen. A variety of chemical mediators are involved in the complex events of inflammation. These mediators may include histamine, serotonin, pros-taglandins, leukotrienes, interleukins, kinins, tumor necrosis factor, and reactive oxygen radicals which originate from inflammatory cells or damaged secretory tissue. Clots formed by the aggregation of leukocytes and blood-clotting factors may block small ducts preventing complete milk removal. Damage to epithelial cells and blockage of small ducts can result in the formation of scar tissue, in some cases with a permanent loss

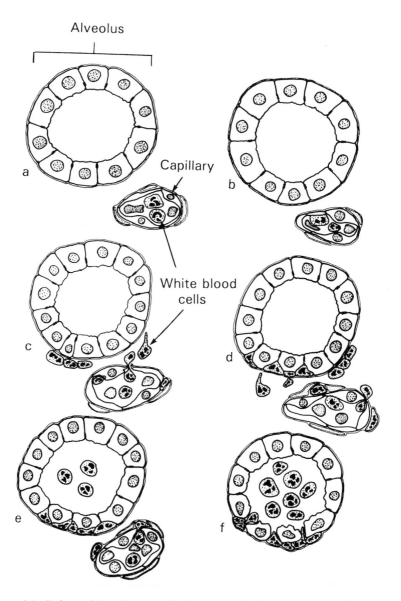

Figure 3.1   Defence of the udder by white blood cells. (a) Normal alveolus and blood vessel; (b) sticking of PMN to vessel wall; (c) migration from capillary and accumulation outside the alveolus; (d) migration through basement membrane and between epithelial cells; (e) accumulation of PMN in lumen and basal epithelial layer; (f) one possible mechanism of crossing the epithelial layer; PMN migration after epithelial cell destruction.

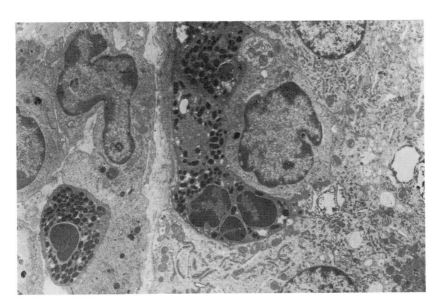

Figure 3.2 Electron micrograph of PMN migrating into infected mammary tissue. (Source: from Harmon and Heald (1982).)

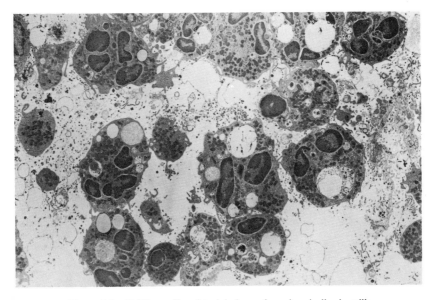

Figure 3.3 PMN engulfing fat globules and casein micelles in milk.

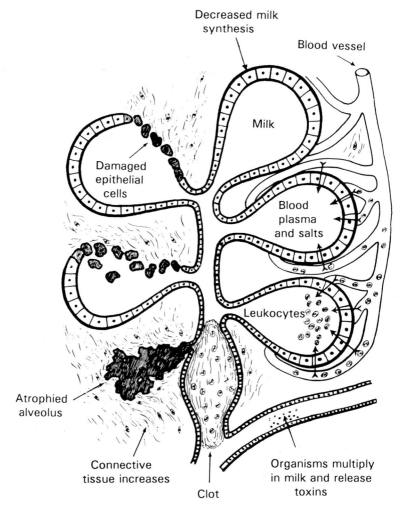

Figure 3.4   Bacterial toxin damage to milk-producing tissue during mastitis.

of function of that portion of the gland. In other cases, inflammation may subside with tissue repair occurring and return of function in that lactation or the subsequent one. The outcome may depend on the causative organism and the severity of the infection.

3.5   Compositional changes

Compositional changes accompany the elevation in SCC and inflammation in an infected mammary gland. Table 3.1 lists examples of some of

Table 3.1 Compositional changes in milk constituents associated with elevated somatic cell counts (SCC)[a]

Constituent	Normal milk (%)	Milk with high SCC (%)	Percent of normal
SNF	8.9	8.8	99
Fat	3.5	3.2	91
Lactose	4.9	4.4	90
Total protein	3.61	3.56	99
Total casein	2.8	2.3	82
Whey protein	0.8	1.3	162
Serum albumin	0.02	0.07	350
Lactoferrin	0.02	0.10	500
Immunoglobulins	0.10	0.60	600
Sodium	0.057	0.105	184
Chloride	0.091	0.147	161
Potassium	0.173	0.157	91
Calcium	0.12	0.04	33

[a]Examples of compositional changes found in various studies. Source: National Mastitis Council (1987) and Kitchen (1981).

the changes in the levels of milk components that accompany mastitis. Mastitis or elevated SCC are associated with a decrease in lactose, α-lactalbumin, and fat in milk because of reduced synthetic activity of the mammary tissue. Some studies have shown no change in fat content, yet total fat yield decreases due to a decline in milk production. There may be some leakage of components such as lactose and α-lactalbumin out of the alveolus between epithelial cells, as these components have been measured in urine or blood of cows with mastitis. Although there may be little change in total protein content, there are dramatic changes in the types of proteins present. The content of casein, the major milk protein of high nutritional quality, and of importance to cheesemakers, declines, but there is an increase in lower quality (for dairy products) whey proteins. Serum albumin, immunoglobulins, transferrin, and other serum proteins pass into milk because of vascular permeability changes. Lactoferrin, the major antibacterial iron-binding protein in mammary secretions, increases in concentration likely due to increased output by the mammary tissue and a minor contribution from PMN.

Mastitis also causes marked changes in the ionic environment and increases in the conductivity of milk. Sodium and chloride increase due to passage from blood into milk. Potassium, normally a significant mineral in milk, declines because of its passage out of milk between damaged epithelial cells. Since most of the calcium in milk is associated with casein, the disruption of casein synthesis contributes to lowered calcium levels in milk.

The pH may increase from a normal of 6.6–6.9 or higher because of movement of blood components into milk. The levels of many enzymes

Table 3.2 Examples of enzymes which may have increased activity in milk as a result of mastitis[a]

Acid phosphatase
α_1-Antitrypsin (antitrypsin or α_1-protease inhibitor)
Alkaline phosphatase
Arylsulphatase
β-Glucuronidase
Catalase
Glutamic-oxaloacetic transaminase (GOT)
Lactate dehydrogenase (LDH)
Lipase
Lysozyme
N-Acetyl-β-D-glucosaminidase (NAGase)
Plasmin
Xanthine oxidase
Various esterases
Various other proteases

[a]Source: Adapted from Kitchen (1981).

and other whey proteins are elevated in milk, originating from damaged tissue, the blood, or leukocytes (Table 3.2). Increased lipase activity and free fatty acids also are found in milk with high SCC. It has been suggested that the lysosomal enzyme N-acetyl-β-D-glucosaminidase (NAGase) is an indicator of tissue damage during mastitis.

Time- and temperature-dependent milk protein breakdown can occur in milk from cows with clinical or subclinical mastitis due to proteolytic enzymes. One important proteolytic enzyme in milk with high SCC is plasmin. Plasmin is normally found in milk, however, there may be more than two-fold increases in its activity in milk during mastitis. Plasminogen, the inactive precursor to plasmin, is the form normally found in plasma. Upon a series of proteolytic cleavages, plasminogen is converted to the active form of plasmin. It is believed that activation occurs in the lumen of the alveolus or early in the process of milk synthesis. Plasmin and somatic cell-derived enzymes can cause extensive damage to casein in the udder before milk removal. One study showed an approximately 20% drop in the intact casein content in fresh raw milk due to proteolysis during *Streptococcus agalactiae* infections. The nature of casein damage caused by plasmin is different from that caused by other proteolytic enzymes. Although the rate of plasmin-related casein breakdown is slower at refrigeration temperatures, plasmin is extremely heat stable. Normal milk pasteurization times and temperatures are not adequate to inactivate elevated plasmin activities in abnormal milk. Thus, deterioration of milk protein as a result of mastitis may continue during processing and storage, and further activation of plasmin may continue.

Because of a strong relationship between some of the inflammatory or compositional changes in milk and the presence of infection, the measure-

Table 3.3 Estimated infection prevalence and losses in milk production associated with elevated bulk tank somatic cell count (SCC)

Bulk tank SCC ($\times 10^3$/ml)	Infected mammary quarters in herd (%)	Production loss[a] (%)
200	6	0
500	16	6
1000	32	18
1500	48	29

[a]Production loss calculated as a percent of production expected at 200 000 cells/ml. Source: Eberhart et al. (1982).

ment of certain components has been used to monitor udder health and, thus, milk quality. Milk SCC probably has been most widely used as a measure of milk quality worldwide due to the development of rapid, electronic cell counting techniques. Other proposed screening tests or tests to monitor the course of infections have included the measurement of catalase, NAGase, antitrypsin, chloride, sodium, and serum albumin levels in milk.

The impact of mastitis on the bacteriological quality of milk and the importance of maintaining a milk supply free of antibiotic residues will be addressed in chapter 8.

3.6   Milk losses

Normal milk, i.e. milk from uninfected mammary glands, will have SCC less than 200 000 cells/ml. Many uninfected cows may have milk SCC below 100 000 cells/ml. An elevation of SCC above this level indicates inflammation in the udder. Many estimates of milk production losses associated with increased SCC have been made. Although the precise values may vary, there exists a strong relationship between increased somatic cell count and milk production loss at the herd level (bulk tank SCC) or at the individual cow level. At the mammary quarter level, losses in infected glands have been found to range from 3 to 50 % of potential milk production. The greatest losses would be expected to occur at the highest SCC. Estimates of losses based on bucket or weigh jar milk (total milk for one cow) are reported to be 6–25 %. Table 3.3 demonstrates that as the proportion of mammary quarters that are infected in a herd increases, the bulk tank or herd SCC also increases. Likewise, as the SCC increases, the level of lost milk production in the herd increases. If the herd or bulk tank SCC reaches 1 000 000 cells/ml, the herd is experiencing about 18% decrease in milk production due to mastitis. These losses hold true for subclinical as well as clinical infections. The losses estimated in Table 3.3 may be conservative, since production losses were calculated as

Table 3.4 Estimated differences in lactation milk yield associated with an increase in somatic cell count (SCC) score

Lactation average score	Average SCC ($\times 10^3$/ml)	Difference in milk yield[a]	
		Lactation 1 (lbs[b]/305 days)	Lactation 2 (lbs[b]/305 days)
0	12.5	—	—
1	25	—	—
2	50	—	—
3	100	−200	−400
4	200	−400	−800
5	400	−600	−1200
6	800	−800	−1600
7	1600	−1000	−2000

[a]Comparisons are with lactation yields at SCC scores of 2. Source: Raubertas and Shook (1982).
[b]1 lb $\approx$ 0.45 kg.

a percentage of production at SCC of 200 000 and an average of 6% of quarters were infected in these herds.

The Dairy Herd Improvement (DHI) Association in the USA has adopted an SCC scoring system that divides the SCC of composite milk into 10 categories from 0 to 9; these are known as linear scores. Table 3.4 shows that for every increase of 1 in the SCC score, the corresponding cell count doubles. In DHI programs, SCC are performed on each milking cow each month, but the average linear SCC score over the lactation more accurately reflects reduced milk yield. Research shows that cows with higher lactation average SCC scores produce less milk (Table 3.4). In addition, the production losses in older cows are about double those of first lactation cows. For every increase of 1 in the SCC score (above 2) there was an additional *decrease* of 400 lbs (1 lb $\approx$ 0.45 kg) of milk for the lactation in older cows. Thus, a linear relationship between SCC score and milk loss was demonstrated. Although it is difficult to estimate precisely the amount of milk lost at a specific SCC, these examples demonstate that elevated SCC due to mastitis result in major losses to the dairy farmer.

3.7 Impact on dairy products

In addition to the economic impact of mastitis on farmers, mastitis causes important and costly losses to processors due to its effect on milk constituents resulting from the many factors discussed earlier in this chapter. Even with the mixing of various sources of bulk milks in large silos, the final milk available to the processor may not be suitable to the manufacture of a particular dairy product. Dairy product manufacturers have become more concerned about the impact of raw milk quality on finished product quality or on the manufacturing process itself. Many milk handlers or processors now offer various types of milk quality premium payment programs, and most of these programs place heavy emphasis on lowering milk SCC.

High levels of free fatty acids produced by the action of lipase on milk fat result in milk and dairy products with off-flavors characterized as rancid flavors. Rancid flavors can be detected in herd milk with SCC as low as 400 000 cells/ml. The free fatty acid content of raw milk with high SCC increases more rapidly than that of low SCC milk. Research has shown that the susceptibility of milk fat to lipase attack is greater in high SCC milk than in low SCC milk. The problem of rancid flavors will be most apparent in high-fat products or products with mild flavors such as butter, cream cheese, spreads, or mild cheeses. The use of low-quality milk in manufacturing may also lead to a more rapid rate of deterioration of flavor during marketing of the product. The shelf-life of market milk is also affected by the use of milk with elevated SCC. It has been shown that the storage stability (5°C) or flavor quality of pasteurized milk decreases as the SCC of the original raw milk increases.

The compositional changes in milk due to mastitis directly affect the quality and yield of cheese. Increased proteolytic activity in milk causes the breaking of the original long amino acid chains of the caseins into smaller fragments. Milk casein does not coagulate properly during cheesemaking, and some small casein fragments and an increased amount of fat are lost into cheese whey causing decreased cheese yields. One hundred pounds of milk yields about 10 lbs of cheese. A loss of 0.31 lb (3.1%) of cheese per 100 lbs of milk was observed with herd milk at the SCC level of 640 000/ml compared with 240 000. Thus, for every 300 000 lbs of milk processed, the loss would be 930 lbs of cheese.

Increased pH, sodium, and chloride adversely affect rennet coagulation and raise labour costs because of longer cheesemaking times. Cheese made from high SCC milk has a high incidence of unclean flavors, pasty textures, and increased moisture content. This cheese generally will be of inferior quality and will be downgraded, which will result in lower returns to manufacturers.

A high level of free fatty acids and increased levels of antibacterial proteins may be inhibitory to starter cultures used in making fermented dairy products. Protein breakdown could cause the body of cultured products such as yogurt to be weak, resulting in undesirable separation of the yogurt into curd and whey in the package. Low-quality milk has an altered maximum heat stability. This property is important to the quality of recombined evaporated or sweetened condensed milk manufactured from milk powder. The functional characteristics (foam stability, gel strength, heat stability) of the milk proteins in condensed and dried milk products can change due to proteolysis. Since condensed and dried milk products are used as ingredients in other foods, changes in milk protein functionality or increased levels of heat resistant plasmin may cause problems for other food processors using these milk products in formulated foods.

3.8   Control of mastitis

Bacteria causing mastitis come from infected cows or quarters, contaminated milking equipment, or from bedding and other environmental sources. To control mastitis a farmer should adopt the following practices.

- *Use proper milking procedure*
  Milk teats that are clean, dry, and free of residue. Wash teats with a sanitizing solution before milking and dry thoroughly with individual paper towels. Attach milking units within 1 min of stimulation, adjust to prevent liner slips, and shut off vacuum to the unit before removal from the cow.
- *Disinfect teats*
  Teat canals may remain somewhat dilated for up to 2 h after milking. A proprietary teat dip or spray should be applied immediately after milking to kill bacteria on the skin surface and prevent infections.
- *Use dry cow therapy*
  Dry cow therapy of each quarter of all cows ensures a longer retention time for antibiotic within the udder with reduced concern for residues in saleable milk. This and the higher concentration of antibiotic used make it more effective than lactating cow therapy in curing infections. Dry cow therapy has the added benefit of preventing new infections early in the dry period.
- *Maintain clean, dry environment*
  Since many of the mastitis-causing bacteria are found in the environment, it is of paramount importance to reduce exposure to these pathogens by providing cows with a clean, dry, stress-free environment. Manure should be removed from concrete yards daily, and bedding in cattle sheds should be clean and plentiful. Sound environmental management applies to dry cows and heifers, because the udder is particularly susceptible to new infection in the early and late dry period.
- *Regularly check milking equipment*
  Milking equipment should be checked every 6 months to rectify faults since insufficient vacuum reserve, improper pulsation and liner slippage may contribute to new infections.

- *Detect, treat and record clinical cases*
  Early detection of clinical mastitis using a strip cup or in-line detectors helps identify candidates for lactation therapy. Records are important in evaluating efficacy of control programs and animals that should be culled.
- *Culling*
  A sound culling policy is recommended to remove persistent offenders from the herd. Hence, records of treatments and individual cow somatic cell counts, available from DHI programs, should be kept for all animals within the herd.

3.9 Measurement

Whilst changes in the physical condition or appearance of the udder or milk have been considered as means of indicating mastitis, they are generally only reliable as indicators of clinical mastitis. The most commonly used technique for indicating mastitis is to measure the SCC of milk. Inflammation of the mammary gland resulting from bacterial infection of the udder results in white blood cells or leukocytes migrating into the milk to fight infection. Hence, a raised somatic cell count is used to signal mastitis. There are three commonly used techniques to measure SCC in milk. The reference method is the direct microscopic count in which somatic cell nuclei are stained with methylene blue and counted. A 0.01 ml aliquot of milk is spread on a 1 cm^2 area of a slide, dried, and stained, and subsequently the stained cells are counted. The method is somewhat tedious and variable.

The Coulter counter method relies on electronic counting of large particle, formalin-fixed somatic cells as the milk passes through an aperture located between electrodes. As each particle (cell) passes through the aperture, a voltage pulse is created and recorded as a count. This method has largely been replaced by the fluoro-optical electronic methods such as Fossomatic.

Milk is mixed with buffer and a fluorescent dye which stains the DNA of the nuclei of somatic cells. The mixture is applied as a microscopically thin film on a rotating disk, and each stained cell is excited with a high-energy lamp. The emitted light energy is detected electronically to give a direct reading of the number of cells per milliliter of milk. Cell count standards are available for calibration control of instruments.

3.10 Summary

Mastitis results in marked reduction in the amount of milk synthesized and in changes in the levels of specific components in milk that reduce the overall milk quality. To the producer this means lower returns because of decreased milk yield and the failure to qualify for quality incentive bonuses. To the processor, it means numerous problems in processing, reduced yield of product, and poor product quality and stability. The production of quality dairy products begins on the farm and continues through processing to proper handling of the product by the consumer. Milk quality problems originating on the farm cannot be eliminated by processing. In fact some of the quality problems may continue or be magnified during processing and after the milk has reached a finished product. The adequate control of mastitis in the dairy herd is one measure to help achieve higher returns for the producer and the processor and to enhance the production of high-quality dairy products.

Further reading

Barbano, D.M. (1989) Impact of mastitis on dairy product quality and yield: Research update. In *Proc. 28th Ann. Meeting Nat. Mastitis Council*. National Mastitis Council, Arlington, VA, USA, p. 44.

Dohoo, I.R. and Meek, A.H. (1982) Somatic cell counts in bovine milk. *Can. Vet. J.*, **23**, 119.

Eberhart, R.J., Gilmore, H.C., Hutchinson, L.J. and Spencer, S.B. (1979) Somatic cell counts in DHI samples. In *Proc. 18th Ann. Meeting Nat. Mastitis Council*. National Mastitis Council, Arlington, VA, USA, p. 32.

Eberhart, R.J., Hutchinson, L.J. and Spencer, S.B. (1982) Relationships of bulk tank somatic cell counts to prevalence of intramammary infection and to indices of herd production. *J. Food Prot.*, **45**, 1125.

Eberhart, R.J., Harmon, R.J., Jasper D.E., Natzke, R.P., Nickerson, S.C., Reneau, J.K., Row, E.H., Smith, K.L. and Spencer, S.B. (1987) *Current Concepts of Bovine Mastitis* (3rd edn). National Mastitis Council, Arlington, VA, USA.

Harmon, R.J. and Heald, C.W. (1982) Migration of polymorphonuclear leucocytes into the bovine mammary gland during experimentally induced *Staphylococcus aureus* mastitis. *Am. J. Vet. Res.*, **43**, 992.

Harmon, R.J. and Langlois, B.E. (1986) Prevalence of minor pathogens and associated somatic cell counts. In *Proc. 25th Ann. Meeting. Nat. Mastitis Council*. National Mastitis Council, Arlington, VA, USA, p. 11.

Kitchen, B.J. (1981) Review of progress of dairy science: Bovine mastitis: milk compositional changes and related diagnostic tests. *J. Dairy Res.*, **48**, 167.

Larson, B.L. (ed.) (1985) *Lactation*. Iowa State University Press, Ames, IA, USA.

Mattila, T. (1985) Diagnostic problems in bovine mastitis, with special reference to new applications of milk antitrypsin, NAGase and bacterial growth. PhD dissertation, College of Veterinary Medicine, Helsinki, Finland.

Mattila, T., Saari, S., Varriala, H. and Sandholm, M. (1985) Milk antitrypsin as a marker of bovine mastitis – correlation with bacteriology. *J. Dairy Sci.*, **68**, 114.

Miller, R.H. and Paape, M.J. (1985) Relationship between milk somatic cell count and milk yield. In *Proc. 24th Ann. Meeting Nat. Mastitis Council*. National Mastitis Council, Arlington, VA, USA.

Newbould, F.H.S. (1974) Microbial diseases of the mammary gland. In *Lactation* (Vol. II) (eds Larson, B.L. and Smith, V.R.). Academic Press, New York, USA, p. 269.

Raubertas, R.F. and Shook, G.E. (1982). Relationship between lactation measures of somatic cell concentration and milk yield. *J. Dairy Sci.*, **65**, 419.

Reneau, J.K. (1986) Effective use of dairy herd improvement somatic cell counts in mastitis control. *J. Dairy Sci.*, **69**, 1708.

Reneau, J.K. and Packard, V.S. (1991) Monitoring mastitis, milk quality and economic losses in dairy fields. *Dairy Food Environ. Sanitarian*, **11**, 4.

Saeman, A.I., Verdi, R.J., Galton, D.M. and Barbano, D.M. (1988) Effect of mastitis on proteolytic activity in bovine milk. *J. Dairy Sci.*, **71**, 505.

Schultz, L.H. (1977) Somatic cells in milk—Physiological aspects and relationship to amount and composition of milk. *J. Food Prot.*, **40**, 125.

Shuster, D.E., Harmon, R.J. Jackson, J.A. and Hemken, R.W. (1991) Suppression of milk production during endotoxin-induced mastitis. *J. Dairy Sci.*, **74**, 3763.

Smith, K.L., Todhunter, D.A. and Schoenberger, P.S. (1985) Environmental mastitis: cause, prevalence, prevention. *J. Dairy Sci.*, **68**, 1531.

Verdi, R.J. and Barbano, D.M. (1991) Effect of coagulants, somatic cell enzymes, and extra-cellular bacterial enzymes on plasminogen activation. *J. Dairy Sci.*, **74**, 772.

4 Hygienic quality

F. HARDING

4.1 Milk production, plant cleaning, on-farm storage and collection of milk

4.1.1 Milk production

Milk, when it leaves the healthy udder, is relatively free from bacteria. While some contamination with bacteria from the milking environment and equipment is inevitable, the total bacterial count of cooled milk, produced under good hygienic conditions, should be lower than 10 000 bacteria/ml. If the bacterial count of milk were allowed to increase significantly, e.g. to over 3 million/ml this could lead to significant degradation of the fat, protein or lactose causing off-flavours and would significantly reduce the flexibility the processor has with respect to storage and use of milk.

In order to achieve a high bacteriological quality at farm level it is important for farmers to be aware of the sources of contamination and to understand how they can be controlled.

The major sources of contamination are the interior and exterior of the udder and the milking equipment.

Mastitic cows can produce milk with very high bacterial counts. Milk from individual cows may contain millions of organisms per millilitre of milk and be so infected that if allowed to go into the bulk vat the herd bulk supply can be elevated to well over 100 000 organisms/ml. The control of mastitis is therefore important with respect to the bacterial count of milk. The udder exterior is also important. Dirty teats may contribute up to 100 000 bacteria/ml.

Contaminated milking equipment is often the major source of bacteria in milk. Visually clean surfaces, because of the high milk volume to plant surface area, should not contribute more than 1000 bacteria/ml of milk. However, surfaces ineffectively cleaned and sterilised or plant containing old milk residues will elevate the bulk milk count by at least 10 000/ml. Careful attention to milk production techniques and plant cleaning is therefore essential if the bulk milk bacterial count is to be kept low. (Figure 4.1).

In order to produce milk of a high hygienic standard the milker must prepare the cow thoroughly before milking, adopt a good milking technique and use a good post-milking routine.

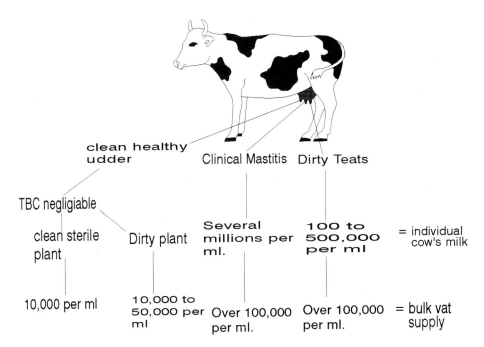

Figure 4.1 Sources of bacterial contamination during milk production.

As stated in chapter 2 preparation of the cow involves adequate stimulation of the milk 'let-down' hormone oxytocin since this facilitates the speed and efficient withdrawal of milk from the udder. Oxytocin is stimulated by handling and washing or dry wiping of the udder, which the cow automatically associates with being milked. Most of the dirt and soiling material which contains bacteria is removed from the udder at this stage. Regular clipping of the hair on the cow's udder and flanks will make udder preparation easier.

The foremilk should be drawn off into a strip cup before milking to check that there are no mastitic clots. Foremilk should not be discarded onto the floor or bedding as this may risk spreading mastitis. Foremilk is likely to have a high bacterial count by virtue of bacteria entering the teat canal and should be drawn off and rejected. In-line mesh filters may be used in machine milking systems to remove sediment and will show mastitis clots but it should be borne in mind that whilst filters remove large particulate material, bacteria associated with it will pass through the filters into the bulk tank.

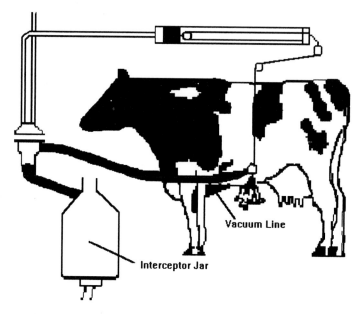

Figure 4.2   Use of milking machine interceptor vessel during milking.

Damaged teats can affect milk quality in that any break in the skin can become a reservoir for mastitic bacteria and give rise to a significant increase in bacterial count. Physical injury to teats is usually caused by cows treading on their own teats, usually due to poor housing design, rough concrete, high cubicle steps, narrow cubicles or overcrowding. It can result in mastitis and in severe cases, blood being drawn into the milk supply during milking.

Hand milking used to be common on very small farms whereas nowadays most farms, especially medium to large farms, tend to use milking machines which suck milk out of the teats by vacuum. Once the cow has been prepared, the teat cups are applied and milking usually takes about 6 min. Care must be taken not to drop clusters and suck up dirt when they are being applied as this will increase the sediment and bacterial count of milk. Milk from individual animals may be collected initially in an interceptor vessel (Figure 4.2) so that milk from newly calved cows, cows with mastitis, cows with damaged teats or cows that have been treated by antibiotics can be kept out of the bulk vat; this milk can be discarded or be used for stock feed. In parlours with recorder jars, visual detection and rejection of abnormal milk is made easier. Such vessels also allow for sampling and yield recording of individual cow's milk.

Milk once collected is either poured into churns through a muslin filter or transferred by vacuum line to a churn collection point or to a bulk vat where it is cooled.

4.1.2   Plant cleaning and sterilisation

Having limited the number of bacteria entering milk during milking, it is essential that contamination from equipment situated between the cow and the refrigerated storage unit is kept to a minimum. Bacteria are present in the air, dust and water—especially any water containing traces of milk residues which may have been left in the milking plant overnight, as such residues provide a very good source of food for bacteria enabling the bacterial counts to increase rapidly.

Dirt and dung harbour large numbers of bacteria, hence the first action in cleaning the plant is to remove all foreign matter from teat cups, etc. using water or detergent. Warm water and alkaline detergents liquefy and emulsify fats which are difficult to remove when cold; however, over time heat and alkaline conditions can cause deposition of protein and calcium salts (milkstone) which need to be removed by periodic acid washes. Cleaning regimes are therefore based on removing visible dirt, removing milk residues (fat, protein and milkstone) which harbour bacteria, then sterilisation of the cleaned surfaces using heat or chemical sterilants such as sodium hypochlorite.

The principle of cleaning and sterilisation involves

- pre-rinse of plant to remove dirt and milk residues using clean potable water;
- detergent wash circulated;
- rinse using potable water;
- disinfectant rinse circulated; and
- final rinse using potable water.

Circulation in place (CIP) cleaning systems using prescribed detergent/sterilants are recommended and achieve a high level of hygiene. Care should be taken to manually clean areas such as the inside covers of the bulk vats which are difficult to clean 'in place'.

It is essential also that only approved chemical disinfectants are used, as non-approved chemicals could leave residues in milk which can cause taints (chapter 5) and may result in rejection of the bulk consignment of milk.

4.1.3   Effect of storage time and temperature on bacterial count

The multiplication of bacteria in milk is dependent on both the temperature and time of storage. The storage temperature also influences the types of bacteria which grow and their spoilage characteristics. The growth rate

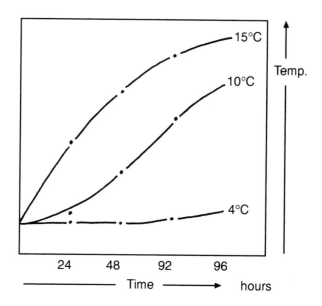

Figure 4.3 Bacterial growth related to milk storage temperature.

of bacteria decreases the lower the storage temperature, and whilst bacterial numbers increase rapidly at 10°C and above, the growth rate of most contaminating bacteria is virtually zero at below 2°C (Figure 4.3).

4.2   Types of bacteria

There are many different microorganisms (mainly bacteria) which can find access to milk and there are three broad temperature ranges classifying their optimum growth rates. Organisms with an optimum growth rate at low temperatures (0–15°C) are the psychrophiles, at medium temperatures (20–40°C) are called the mesophiles and at high temperatures (45–55°C) the thermophiles. These do not represent absolute cut-off points, but are general groupings, for example, whilst mesophiles grow best in the medium temperature range some may still grow at the lower temperature range.

   Psychrotrophic bacteria can grow at refrigeration temperatures. These are of interest to those storing milk at low temperatures. These bacteria grow slowly and mostly feed by breaking down proteins (proteolysis) and fats (lipolysis). They can develop in raw milk during cold storage, and high numbers (in excess of 3 million/ml) can produce enough enzymes to cause flavour defects. The psychrotrophic bacteria are killed by pasteurisation, however the enzymes they produce can survive. This problem

$$C_{12}H_{22}O_{11} + H_2O \longrightarrow C_6H_{12}O_6 + C_6H_{12}O_6$$

Lactose   Glucose   Galactose

$$2C_6H_{12}O_6 \longrightarrow 4CH_3COCOOH$$

Pyruvic acid

$$4CH_3COCOOH \longrightarrow 4CH_3CHOH\text{-}COOH + 36.4\,kCal$$

Lactic acid

Figure 4.4   Conversion of lactose to lactic acid.

occurs mainly in UHT milk which is stored at ambient temperatures for several months (chapter 8). The most active psychrotrophs are Gram-negative rods such as *Pseudomonas* spp.

Measurement of bacterial numbers in milk is of interest because of their direct role in milk spoilage and because they are indicators of poor hygienic production or ineffective pasteurisation of milk.

Mesophilic bacteria are the group which grow best at 'normal' temperatures ranging from about 20 to 40°C. They are typified by the lactobacilli which can attack the milk sugar lactose and convert it to lactic acid (Figure 4.4). Their uncontrolled growth gives rise to the souring and even curdling of milk stored at ambient temperatures.

There are some sporeforming bacteria (usually *Bacillus* species) which are also psychrotrophic and these bacterial spores can survive pasteurisation then germinate to grow in the pasteurised milk, ultimately causing spoilage of the finished product.

Thermoduric bacteria as the name states can endure heat and are defined as the organisms which survive pasteurisation, i.e. laboratory heating to 60°C for 60 min.

4.3   Cooling and storage of milk on the farm

When milk leaves the cow it is virtually free from bacteria and its temperature is about 37°C. Although careful milking conditions will result in

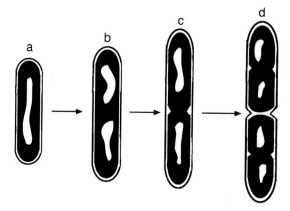

Figure 4.5 Multiplication of bacteria by binary fission. (a) Cell prior to division; (b) to (d) successive stages of division.

limited bacterial contamination, it is impossible to keep all microorganisms out hence it is important to limit their multiplication. Bacteria multiply by binary fission (Figure 4.5) and in favourable conditions at high temperatures fission can occur every 20–30 min; hence in 0.5 h one cell becomes two, in 1 h 4, in 1.5 h 8, in 2 h 16, etc. until in as little as 12 h one cell has become well over 10 million viable cells. Milk must therefore be cooled as soon as possible after milking to a temperature below 4°C in order to minimise bacterial growth.

Cold water, chilled water or preferably refrigerated units may be used for cooling milk. Immersion coolers with chilled water circulation are often used for churn milk. Where milking machines and refrigerated bulk farm tanks are used, an ice bank in the bulk vat very rapidly cools milk to below 4°C.

4.4 Collection, delivery and reception of milk

The frequency at which milk should be collected depends on the on-farm storage capacity and the refrigeration temperatures which can be achieved. Clearly, there are potential transport cost savings to be made by less frequent collection of milk. Whilst it is possible to store milk for 7 days at 1.5–2°C, providing the initial quality is excellent, holding milk on farm for this length of time is not usual. In practice, milk produced under good hygiene conditions is stored for collection every 3 days or every 2 days with the more costly alternative of every day collection becoming less common.

Experiments have taken place in some countries to concentrate milk on the farm by evaporation or ultrafiltration; however, such practices have found limited appeal due to high capital cost of equipment and the strict hygienic control required to maintain the processing plant on the farm.

4.4.1 Churn collection

Cooled milk in churns or cans is usually taken to a convenient collection point just before the collection vehicle arrives. Churns should be protected from sunshine and are usually taken to collection centres where milk in each individual churn is inspected and, providing the milk is acceptable, the volume is measured and recorded, samples are taken and the churns are emptied into a bulk vessel for cooling and storage or for immediate heat treatment.

4.4.2 Bulk collection

Milk stored in refrigerated bulks vat is collected by being pumped into a tanker, after the tanker driver has checked the temperature and assured himself by sight and smell that the milk is satisfactory. The milk volume will have been measured by a calibrated dipstick or more normally by use of an automatic flow meter on the collection vehicle. Automatic recording of the milk volume together with other data such as temperature is becoming more common using microcomputers on the collection vehicles. Automatic data capture provides a collection ticket, a copy of which is left with the producer, and data on magnetic tape which can be automatically transmitted to the collection centre computer. Since the individual farm supply will be blended in the tanker together with supplies from other farms, it is desirable to take samples of each consignment at point of collection in order to enable faults to be traced back to source, should there be any problems with the quality of the milk in the tanker.

4.5 Delivery and storage prior to processing

The tanker, having collected milk from its allocated farms, will then deliver it to the creamery or dairy. The tanker contents will normally be sampled on receipt, the milk inspected by smell and taste (after laboratory pasteurisation) and tested by rapid techniques to ensure the milk is of an acceptable quality. This regular quality inspection 'down the chain' is important since the volume and value of milk at risk increases significantly at each pooling step (Table 4.1):

When the tanker of milk is accepted it is pumped into a silo where it may be used within a few hours or be stored for future use.

Table 4.1   Increase in volume at risk the later a defect is found

	Cow	Vat	Tanker	Silo
Litres of milk at risk	15.5	92.5	9000	90 000

4.5.1   Storage of milk prior to processing

Where milk is to be stored before being pasteurised, bacteriological spoilage can best be minimised by keeping milk cool, preferably at a temperature below 4°C. If milk is to be stored for long periods deep cooling to 2°C is recommended.

The addition of carbon dioxide has been shown to lengthen the storage period of milk held at low temperatures by 3 days, since the bicarbonate ion produced is toxic to psychrotrophic bacteria. The carbon dioxide can be removed under vacuum prior to processing.

In countries where cooling may prove difficult, glucose oxidase or xanthanine oxidase may be added to activate the lactoperoxidase system of milk and hence generate hydrogen peroxide which acts as a bacteriostat.

Another approach has been to preserve milk to be used in cheesemaking by adding starter cultures to the cold stored milk. Although the starter cultures, which thrive and grow best at mesophilic temperatures, do not grow, they are present in sufficient numbers to inhibit the growth of the psychrotrophic organisms, thereby extending the shelf-life of the milk being stored until cheesemaking can start.

In some countries thermisation is used to extend prepasteurisation storage life. Thermisation involves heat treating milk to 60–66°C for about 15 s, this being below pasteurisation conditions. Thermisation must not, however, be considered as a salvage technique since bacterial damage may already have taken place if milk has very high bacterial counts. It does, however, reduce bacterial numbers, hence extending the amount of time milk can be stored prior to it being processed. Thermisation followed by deep cooling has been shown to be suitable for holding milk for up to 7 days before processing without there being a major impact on product quality.

4.6   Importance of hygienic quality of milk

Milk is an ideal balanced food for man; it is not surprising therefore that it also provides an ideal medium for growth of bacteria. We use this fact in harnessing bacteria as starter cultures for cheese, yogurt and fermented milks where, by selecting the bacteria we use, we can predict their effect.

Bacteria finding accidental access to milk may give rise to consumer health problems or product faults. As stated earlier bacteria may produce enzymes which attack fat, protein or lactose and some of these enzymes even survive in milk after the bacteria have been killed by heat treatment. Additionally, some bacteria such as *Bacillus* and *Clostridium* spp. are able to live in 'suspended animation' by forming spores. These spores are like a protective shell which enable the organism to survive hostile conditions likely to kill normal vegetative bacteria. Spores survive pasteurisation, after which, under good growth conditions, they revert to the vegetative state by germinating, then can grow and adversely affect the quality of milk.

The damage high numbers can do to milk prior to processing, the numbers of heat stable enzymes they can produce, and the number of thermoduric bacteria which may survive pasteurisation, hence affecting the quality of the pasteurised product, can all be minimised by starting the manufacturing process with raw milk of good hygienic quality.

The hygienic quality of milk at the point of production is also of importance from both public health and consumer perception points of view, making it important for milk to be produced with a low bacterial count and the count, by adequate temperature control, is to be kept low until the point of processing.

4.7 Measurement of the hygienic quality of milk

The general appearance, cleanliness, colour and smell of farm milk should be checked at collection before it is blended with milk from other suppliers, since the volume and value at risk increases down the chain.

Where milk is to be checked for taint (taste) (chapter 5), normally before off-loading, the sample should be laboratory pasteurised (heated to 63.3°C for 35 min, then cooled) before tasting in order to ensure that any pathogens present are killed. Laboratory pasteurisation can be achieved by heating milk held in a test tube in a waterbath, or in a microwave oven. It is important that the milk is held at the required temperature for the full time to effectively kill vegetative pathogens.

For milk collected in churns at temperatures of 10–15°C or higher, bacterial spoilage will be due to lactic acid production; hence, the quality control tests used are focused on measuring this spoilage step. Milk has a natural acidity produced by buffering salts. The developed acidity (lactic acid) is negligible in fresh milk and rises as bacterial action attacks lactose.

4.7.1 Simple, rapid tests for mesophiles

The 'clot on boiling' test involves heating a small volume of milk to boiling point in a test tube. If the milk has developed about 0.1% lactic acid it will clot and should be rejected. The test is quick, cheap and easy to operate; however, it is relatively insensitive in that milk failing the test will be in an advanced state of souring.

A slightly more sensitive test is the alcohol stability test in which 3 ml of milk is shaken with 3 ml of alcohol in a graduated test tube. If no flocculation occurs a further 3 ml of alcohol is added. The absence of flocculation after addition of 6 ml of alcohol shows milk to have an acceptably low developed acidity. The alcohol acts by dehydrating and denaturing milk proteins. Positive results are obtained with colostrum or near-sour milks. The test can give false positives where mineral imbalance of the milk rather than developed acidity can be the cause of flocculation.

A further test for the by-product of bacterial action is the titratable acidity test in which 10 ml of milk is titrated with 1/9 normal sodium hydroxide against a phenolphthalein indicator. The molecular weight of lactic acid is 90, hence each ml of N/9 sodium hydroxide corresponds to 0.01 g lactic acid. As the natural acidity of normal milk is less than 0.16% lactic acid equivalent, this figure is normally subtracted from the calculated percent lactic acid in order to give a measure of 'developed acidity'.

The above methods give a measure of developed acidity, i.e. the damage mesophilic bacteria have already done. Since mesophilic bacteria change the redox potential of milk they will reduce dyes such as methylene blue and resazurin which change colour; hence these can be used as an indication of microbial activity. Quick reduction of the dyes shows a high microbial activity and vice versa. Dye reduction tests are simple in that they only involve incubation of 9 ml of milk and 1 ml of the dye in a sterile stoppered test tube at 37.5°C, the optimum temperature for mesophiles, followed by visual checking of the tube.

The tubes are checked every 30 min for decoloration and in general the time taken for complete reduction is inversely proportional to the number of bacteria in the milk. The tests however are imprecise, as some bacteria have a high rate of reduction and others low; additionally somatic cells can also reduce the dyes. These tests are, however, cheap, easy to operate and offer a useful general grading method for the hygienic quality of milk that has not been refrigerated.

4.7.2   Tests for cooled milk

The above tests offer simple means of indicating the hygienic quality of milk stored under relatively high temperature conditions, i.e. 8–15°C or above, by indirect measurement of milk spoilage organisms. For milk cooled to below 5°C, the psychrophilic and psychrotrophic organisms grow and different test methods are required. The most widely used test as a general indication of good hygienic production is the total bacterial colony count (TBC), or more correctly called a standard plate count

(SPC) or total viable colony count (TVC) since only the living bacteria capable of forming colonies under the specific conditions used are measured. The TVC however is often referred to as the TBC and is widely used as an indication of the hygienic conditions adopted during milk production even though the bacteria counted may not necessarily themselves cause spoilage directly.

There are many ways of measuring the bacterial content of milk. The direct microscopic count was perhaps the first method to be developed and involves examining stained films of a measured volume of milk dried on a glass slide. Staining allows distinctive shapes of bacteria and somatic cells to be recognised and offers rapid quality assessment within 10–15 min. Although dead cells may lose their stainability compared with viable organisms, differentiation between dead and live organisms is not always easy and the test method demands considerable operational experience. Because of its poor sensitivity the test is not very practical for milk of low bacterial count. Hence, for good quality milk there is a need to grow organisms to increase numbers prior to counting them in order to ensure that the count is reasonably accurate. Preincubation of samples, under controlled conditions, is therefore sometimes used prior to testing good quality raw or pasteurised milk for bacteriological quality.

The SPC method is an empirical method of assessing milk quality. It involves growing bacteria on a gel-like material, agar, which also contains the necessary nutrients to support microbial growth. The procedure involves incubating about 0.01 ml of milk in agar at 30°C for 3 days, after which time the number of colonies formed during incubation are counted. The test is a general indication of cleanliness but has a number of shortcomings. For example, bacteria can be present in milk singly, in pairs, chains or clumps which may be broken up by agitation, yet each may form a colony during incubation. The method of shaking and the degree of breaking of clumps will therefore affect the count recorded. Colonies may grow on top of each other or some bacteria may not grow at all due to the absence of specific nutrient requirement, reaction to oxygen or incubation times and temperatures which may not suit particular organisms. Whilst the test is simple, it is labour intensive, lacks precision and between-laboratory reproducibility is poor. Taking 3 days to produce a result, the test only produces historic information.

In spite of these shortcomings, where a single test method is to be adopted as a measure of good hygiene, the total viable count tends to be used. The reference test method for the SPC involves preparation of serial dilutions of milk in order to transfer the required volume to the Petri dish. An alternative technique is the Thompson loop method in which a standard volume (0.01 ml) of the milk samples is withdrawn using a calibrated loop. This method has been automated to provide mass testing laboratories with a TBC technique for grading individual ex-farm milk supplies.

The objective when deciding what volume of milk to take for incubation is to have between 30 and 300 colonies on the incubated plate. Thus, when the bacterial count is 10 000 organisms/ml of milk, incubation of 0.01 ml of the milk will give 100 colonies on the plate. However, if the count were 100 000 this would result in 1000 colonies on the plate creating overcrowding and making counting difficult. For such milk a smaller volume, i.e. 0.001 ml should be taken. For SPCs where the bacterial count of the milk is not known, it is usual to prepare two or more plates each with 10-fold different volumes of milk in each plate, e.g. 0.01 and 0.001 ml in order to span the range of counts likely to be encountered.

After incubation of the plates for 3 days at 30°C, the number of colonies are counted manually or by an image analyser which automatically scans the plate and counts colonies much more rapidly and accurately than the human eye, once suitably calibrated. Automatic colony counters are calibrated to count colonies of particular sizes thereby removing the question of human discretion. They can also be programmed to compensate for 'spreaders'—a problem created by particular microorganisms which produce colonies which spread widely and cover a large area of the plate making direct manual counting difficult to interpret.

Alternative colony counting systems to the SPC include the roll tube method in which, instead of samples being incubated in a Petri dish, they are incubated in a cylindrical tube. This technique whilst less accurate than the SPC offers advantages of reduced cost and space saving.

The spiral plate counting method is another variation of the SPC in which a spiral plating instrument inoculates the surface of a prepared agar plate in such a way that between 500 and 500 000 bacteria/ml can be counted. The plate deposits a decreasing amount of milk on the surface of the agar plate by means of an Archimedean spiral such that the volume of the sample deposited at any portion of the plate is known. Colonies on a portion of this plate are counted using a special grid which associates a calibrated volume with each area. This technique removes the need for multiple dilutions necessary in the SPC techniques.

Modifications aimed at improving and simplifying sample delivery to the media for growth or for counting colonies have been features of developments aimed at improving the SPC. The 3M petrifilm is one such example. Petrifilm packages the agar plate in a convenient prepack disposable format in which the sample under test is placed in a shallow 6 cm diameter well and sandwiched between two plastic sheets. The sample rehydrates the dehydrated culture medium in the well; this in effect becomes an agar plate which is then counted after incubation in the usual way. Petrifilm test methods are available for total count, coliform count and *Escherichia coli* count.

In recent years there has been a move away from growing and counting bacterial colonies towards techniques involving physical concentration of bacteria, staining, then counting the stained organisms. Since such methods normally remove the need for the 3 day incubation period required for colony growth in the SPC they tend to be referred to as rapid methods.

4.7.3 Staining and counting bacteria

One such rapid method is the DEFT (direct epifluorescent filter technique) in which about 2 ml of milk is treated with trypsin and a surfactant to disperse the fat and cellular debris, etc. The mixture is then passed through a 0.6 μm filter so that bacteria are concentrated on the filter, where they are stained with acridine orange and counted using microscopic techniques. From this, the number of bacteria per ml of milk can be calculated. It is claimed that, since acridine orange is a 'vital stain', dead and alive bacteria stain differently and can be differentially counted by DEFT.

The method is quick (about 20 min) and has a sensitivity of 10^3–10^4 organisms/ml. It is however rather expensive, labour intensive and operators need to be well trained in the test before they can consistently achieve good results. The DEFT test has been automated and other automated methods involving differential staining of bacteria include the Biofoss, the Bactoscan and the Autotrak. The latter involves staining bacteria that have been fixed to a moving magnetic tape.

The Bactoscan is similar in principle to the DEFT test. However, with the Bactoscan, bacteria are separated from the milk constituents and somatic cells by centrifugation then stained by acridine orange. The instrument has been fully automated and is widely used as a means of grading ex-farm milk supplies for payment according to their hygienic quality.

Whereas the SPC does not differentiate between single organisms, pairs and groups (clumps) of bacteria, which are all measured as single colonies, these staining techniques measure only single bacteria hence give higher counts. The relationship between traditional SPC techniques and single cell measuring techniques needs careful interpretation. Since it is individual bacteria that attack milk constituents the measurement of single cells rather than colonies gives a better correlation of count with the impact of bacteria on milk quality.

The techniques described above count bacteria, either after growing them into countable colonies or by staining the individual bacterial cells. These are called direct counting techniques. A growing number of techniques either measure components of the microbial cell or metabolites produced by its activity—these are called the indirect methods of analysis.

4.7.4   Measurement of metabolic products of microbial cells

4.7.4.1   Pyruvate.   Since pyruvic acid is the end-product of glycolysis (Figure 4.4), pyruvate levels in milk increase with increased bacterial numbers.

Measurement involves reduction of pyruvate to lactic acid in the presence of the enzyme lactate dehydrogenase (LDH) obtained from rabbit muscle, with simultaneous oxidation of $NADH_2$. The amount of $NADH_2$ used is equivalent to the pyruvate content, and residual $NADH_2$ is measured spectrophotometrically. Pyruvate is not affected by pasteurisation; hence measurements in pasteurised milk indicate the bacteriological quality of the raw milk used.

Pyruvate determination has also been advocated as a means of measuring post-pasteurisation contamination. The method involves measuring the pyruvate content of freshly pasteurised milk and also that of the same sample after preincubation. The difference in pyruvate concentrations gives a measure of post-pasteurisation contamination.

4.7.4.2   Bioluminescence.   All living cells contain ATP which acts as a substrate in the bioluminescence firefly enzymes system luciferin–luciferase, giving rise to light emission. Thus the very sensitive light emission can be used as a measure of low levels of bacteria via their ATP content.

$$\text{ATP} + \text{luciferin} + \text{oxygen} \xrightarrow{\text{luciferase}} \text{reaction products} + \underline{\text{LIGHT}}$$

There is a problem, however, in that the amount of bacterial ATP in milk is small compared with other sources, such as somatic cells, and these have to be removed before bacterial ATP can be measured. The sensitivity of commercially available test kits is about 10^4 organisms/ml.

The method is not only suitable for indicating total bacterial contamination of milk but has also been used as a rapid measure of bacterial contamination of swabs and rinses used to assess plant cleanliness. The method is also being developed as a measure of protease and lipase enzymes in milk.

4.7.5   Measurement of metabolic activity

The dye reduction tests discussed earlier are the simplest example of measurement of microorganisms through the process of measuring their metabolic activity. There are, however, many others.

Active bacteria produce heat, and microcalorimetry—measuring the small temperature increase of samples—has been suggested as a technique to measure bacterial biomass. It has however not found popularity in the dairy industry.

A number of microbial species produce carbon dioxide from glucose and emission of radioactive carbon dioxide from a ^{14}C-labelled glucose has also been proposed. This radiometric method again has not proved popular in the dairy industry.

A technique which has been taken up by the dairy industry is the measurement of electrical conductivity or impedance. When bacteria digest a substrate they change its electrical resistance. The media used is often similar to that used in traditional methods. However, results can be obtained in 8–18 h—the higher the bacterial load the quicker the test result—since significant changes in impedance of a medium occur when a threshold limit of about 10^6 organisms/ml is reached. The time taken for this to happen is proportional to the bacterial load at the start of the test.

The equipment is expensive, however many tests can be carried out simultaneously. By choosing specific media, different test organisms can be detected by this electrical method.

4.8 The future

A technique used in clinical chemistry may well find itself being used in dairy technology. The technique, flow cytometry, involves measuring the reflection of laser light from a very narrow stream of the fluid under test. Particles in the fluid scatter the light, and the intensity and angle of scatter is measured yielding information about the size and shape of the cell.

The technique is quick, as the count is made in minutes, and dedicated computers interpret the data. The technique is also very sensitive, being capable of counting down to 100 cells/ml. In theory, flow cytometry can measure somatic cells and total bacterial count in the same sample. Using fluorescent dyes to stain specific bacteria it seems possible that flow cytometry could possibly be used to count specific species. The technique therefore might offer promise as a versatile tool for raw milk quality control in the future and is currently being used commercially to detect the presence of yeasts in yogurt.

4.9 Sampling, storage, preservation and transportation of samples

Any measurement of milk quality relies on the sample under test being representative of the bulk supply from which it was drawn and this demands adherence to a correct sampling procedure. Since butterfat is a suspension which readily separates out, all milk to be sampled must be adequately mixed. If milk in a consignment is held in different vessels,

Figure 4.6   Plunger used for mixing milk in churns or tankers.

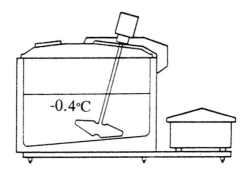

Figure 4.7   Bulk cooling tank with agitator and cooling unit.

such as churns, proportional subsamples must be taken and mixed to provide a master sample which can be conserved until it is tested.

Sampling techniques are described in standard methods (IDF, 1985). Mixing of milk can be achieved by pouring the milk from one container to another, by means of a plunger (Figure 4.6) or mechanical agitation. Thorough mixing is particularly important for cold stored milk and bulk vats on farms are fitted with automatic agitators which not only mix the milk periodically during cooling, but are also used to give a 2 min vigorous mixing prior to a sample being taken (Figure 4.7).

Milk in cans or churns can be mixed by means of a plunger. A graduated dipper is used to draw a representative sample from each churn proportional to its contents, i.e. 8/10th of a sterile dipper for 8 gallons (1 gallon (UK) $\approx$ 4.5 litres) and a full dipper for 10 gallons. Individual churn samples are collected in a sterile jug, mixed and a sample of the composite is then transferred to a clean, dry sterile container upon which the farm name, volume of milk and date should be recorded.

Large plungers are used for reference sampling of milk in static tanks or road tankers which need vigorous mixing for 15 min. Tankers may also be mixed using mechanical agitators lowered into the vessel. However, these sometimes prove difficult to clean and sterilise.

Air agitation is also sometimes used to mix milk in tankers but care needs to be taken to ensure that lipolytic hydrolysis or degradation of milk fat is not induced.

A good method of checking the efficiency of agitation is to take samples from different parts of the container—as far apart as possible and to demonstrate that these give the same butterfat value. Top and bottom samples should be compared for tanker samples, for example, and samples from each corner of the vat should give the same butterfat level for a well mixed bulk vat. In-line samplers are sometimes used to obtain representative samples of a milk intake to a creamery or dairy. These operate by a small positive displacement pump linked to the main pump withdrawing a sample from the intake line every x litres pumped. Tanker-mounted automatic sampling devices are used in some countries for automatic sampling of milk during collection at the farm. However, such systems do not accurately sample unmixed milk, may have a significant 'carry over' from one sample to the next, which can invalidate sensitive tests, and are expensive. For these reasons automatic samplers should be thoroughly evaluated to ensure they meet the specific need.

Samples must be taken into clean, dry, and for microbiological analyses, sterile sample containers. Each should be clearly identified with full details of the sample, the date and preferably the sampler's name. Modern test instruments, capable of automatic data capture can record data directly from bar code labels or magnetic tape thus eliminating risks of human transcription errors.

Once a representative sample has been taken and the container has been adequately identified, the next task is to transport it to the test centre in good condition.

4.9.1 Sample transport and preservation

The ideal way to protect the sample against microbiological spoilage is to maintain it as close to 0°C as possible. For most analyses, freezing should be avoided since it may cause disruption of bacterial cells and may also affect the physical condition of fat. The target temperature range is therefore between 0 and 2°C.

Two cooling systems have been fully evaluated for transporting unpreserved samples to mass testing laboratories. One involves the transportation of samples in iced water and the second involves the use of prefrozen eutectic icepacks.

Both techniques require specially designed insulated boxes and rely on the fact that there is little or no bacterial growth within 24–36 h of sampling, providing samples are held at 2°C or below.

Cold storage and transportation of samples, whilst almost essential for microbiological analysis, is expensive. Hence, if samples are only to be tested for compositional quality consideration can be given to preserving samples using antimicrobial agents.

Chemical preservatives such as potassium dichromate, mercuric chloride (now discontinued for environmental reasons) and sodium azide were once commonly used. Bronopol, a more environmentally friendly preservative which is biodegradable, is now more widely used for transportation of samples at ambient temperature for compositional quality testing.

The sample preservation system chosen will depend on the type of test to be applied and the degree of accuracy demanded. Sample deterioration can take three forms:

(1) Microbiological deterioration occurs because milk is an ideal medium for microbial growth—the higher the temperature the greater the bacterial growth. At 0–2°C microbial numbers will remain virtually unchanged for up to 24–36 h.

(2) Physical deterioration can also occur and samples transported at more than 8°C can 'oil'. Oiling involves the breakdown of fat globule membranes, due to shaking of the samples during transportation. The resulting free fat separates, floats to the top of the sample and is difficult to mix making it imposible to take a representative subsample for test. Instrumental measurement on oiled samples tends to produce low butterfat results because the instrument draws a fat deficient sample from below the oil surface. Transportation of samples at low temperatures (below 6°C) limits or prevents oiling.

(3) Chemical deterioration can also occur involving chemical changes to milk caused by microorganisms. At worst unpreserved milk transported at ambient temperatures will sour, resulting in clotting of the milk making withdrawal of a representative subsample virtually impossible. Before physical coagulation becomes obvious, the sample may change chemically in that bacteria may convert lactose to lactic acid. Such a change will affect solids-not-fat, lactose, freezing point and antibiotic measurements and can affect infrared determinations used for fat, protein and lactose measurement. Cold sample transportation will minimise microbiological, chemical and physical deterioration.

The use of chemical preservatives severely limit the use of samples for microbiological tests, for antibiotic and inhibitory substances tests, and for somatic cell counts. Preservation may also decrease the accuracy of instrumental or chemical analysis and freezing point determination. However, if cold sample transportation is just not possible, chemical preservation using bacteriostats may be used to restrict microbial growth with resultant loss of test reliability.

References and further reading

Adams and Hope (1986) Fast food techniques. *Lab. Practice*, July, 15–18.

Anon (1991) *A Guide to Clean Milk Product*. MAFF Publications, London, UK.

APHA (1978) American Public Health Association, Washington, DC, USA. *Standard Methods for the Examination of Dairy Products*.

Bautista, D.A. *et al.* (1992) The application of ATP-bioluminescence for the assessment of milk quality and factory hygiene. *J. Rapid Meth. Autom. Microbiol.*, **1**, 179–193.

Boros, V. *et al.* (1984) Study of the possibility of preservation of milk samples for microbial examination. *Food Sci. Technol. Abstr.*, **16**(3), 191 (Abstr. 3, p. 827).

Easter, M. (1991) Alternative and rapid microbiological methods. *J. Soc. Dairy Technol.*, **44** (1).

Gilmour, A. and Rowe, M.T. (1990) *Dairy Microbiology* (Vol. 1) (ed. Robinson, R.K.) Elsevier Applied Science, London, UK.

Griffiths, M.W., Banks, J.M., McIntyre, L. and Limond, A. (1991) Some insight into the mechanism of inhibition of psychrotrophic bacterial growth in raw milk by lactic acid bacteria. *J. Soc. Dairy Technol.*, **44**(1), 24–29.

IDF (1980) *Factors Affecting the Bacteriological Quality of Raw Milk* (Document 120). IDF, Brussels, Belgium.

IDF (1984) *Thermisation of Milk—Milk treatment on the Farm (or On-Farm use of Membrane Systems) (Bulletin 182)*. IDF, Brussels, Belgium.

IDF (1988) *Code of Practice for the Preservation of Raw Milk by the Lactoperoxidase System* (Bulletin 234). IDF, Brussels, Belgium.

Juffs, H.S. and Babel, F.J. (1975) Inhibition of psychrotrophic bacteria by lactic cultures in milk stored at low temperatures. *J. Dairy Sci.*, **58**, 1612–1619.

Kreutzer, K. (1981) Preservation of milk samples for examining inhibitory substances. *Food Sci. Technol. Abstr.*, **13**, (9), 142 (Abstr. 9, p. 1591).

Law, B.A. and Mabbitt, L.A. (1983) *Spoilage, Food Microbiology Advances and Prospects*. Academic Press, London, UK, pp. 131–156.

Manners, J.G. (1985). Trends in microbiological testing of milk and dairy products. *Aus. J. Dairy Technol.*, June, 73–75.

Marth, E.H. (1978) *Standard Methods for the Examination of Dairy Products*. American Public Health Institute, Washington, DC, USA.

McCann, G., Moran, L. and Rowe, M. (1991). Rapid methods for microbiological testing. *Milk Industry*, February, 15–16.

O'Connor, F. (1984). Rapid methods for assessing microbiological quality of milk. *Aus. J. Dairy Technol.*, June.

Prentice, G.A. and Neaves, P.J. (1986) The role of micro-organisms in the dairy industry. *Appl. Bacteriol. Symp.* **Supplement**, 435–575.

Reiter, B. and Harnuly, G. (1984) Lactoperoxidase antibacterial system. Natural occurrence biological functions and practical applications. *J. Food. Prot.*, **47**(9), 724–732.

Robinson, R.K. (1991) *Dairy Microbiology* (2nd edn) Elsevier Applied Science, London, UK.

Sally Pownan Reports (1986) Beating the bugs. *Food Manufacture*, August, 22–25.

Stanley, P.E. (1982) Rapid microbiol counting using ATP technology. *Food*, October, 29–34.

Sutherland, A.D. *et al.* (1994) The Biotrace method for estimating bacterial numbers in milk by bioluminescence. *J. Soc. Dairy Technol.*, **47**, 117–120.

Szijarto, L.F., Harding, F., Hill, A.R. and Melichercik, J. (1990) Cooling systems for transport of unpreserved milk samples. *J. Dairy Sci.*, **73**, 2299–2308.

5 Adulteration of milk
F. HARDING

5.1 Introduction

When consumers buy milk they have a right to assume that it will be pure and unadulterated. Hence, there is an obligation on the dairy industry to provide adequate quality control systems. Milk may be adulterated on purpose in order to defraud—fortunately a rare occurrence—or accidentally during production or processing. There are many potential adulterants:

(a) Extraneous water
(b) Detergents/sterilants accidentally finding access to milk during production
(c) Teat dips, udder salves, etc.
(d) Neutralisers used to mask developed acidity
(e) Skim-milk powder used to elevate milk solids
(f) Salt or sugar used to mask extraneous water or to elevate total solids
(g) Preservatives such as formalin, hydrogen peroxide, hypochlorite, etc. used to mask poor hygienic quality
(h) Foreign fats

Since milking plants and process plants are wet cleaned the most common potential adulterant in milk is extraneous water.

5.2 Extraneous Water

Milk is a variable biological fluid, and the fat, protein, lactose and—even the natural water content—all vary from cow to cow and from herd to herd. Compositional quality therefore cannot be used as a measure of the 'purity' of milk. Developing a method of controlling extraneous water in milk has therefore occupied the minds of food control authorities since the mid-1800s.

In spite of the wide variations which occur, compositional quality has been used as an *indication* of adulteration. There is a need to survey milk quality in a specific country before one can set a standard; however a solids-not-fat (SNF) of 8.5% was at one time set as a *presumptive* legal standard in the UK. Whilst this standard did not prove that milk below

8.5% SNF was adulterated nor that milk greater than 8.5% SNF was genuine it did act as a crude indicator enabling the analyst to concentrate on suspect herds.

5.2.1 Vieth ratio

A method which was used with some success in the early 1900s was application of 'The Vieth Ratio'. Dr P. Vieth observed that the ratio of lactose, proteins and ash in the non-fat solids portion of milk was 13 : 9 : 2. For average milk of 4.6% lactose, 3.2% protein, 0.7% ash it can be seen that Vieth's ratio holds good, i.e. 13.14 : 9.14 : 2. Dr Vieth argued that if SNF is depressed by virtue of a low lactose value due to mastitis, for example, then an abnormal Vieth ratio would occur. However, all components, i.e. lactose, protein and ash, would be equally reduced if the low SNF were caused by extraneous water. A low SNF and a normal Vieth ratio is a strong indication of the presence of extraneous water.

5.2.2 Nitrates as an indication of extraneous water

Cow's milk is virtually free from nitrates, even when cows may have ingested them in food or drink. Most waters, on the other hand, contain traces of nitrates. The nitrate test can therefore be used as a qualitative test for extraneous water in milk. It must be emphasised however that a milk which does not contain nitrates cannot be assumed to be free from extraneous water.

The Gerber method may give an indication of the presence of nitrites or nitrates since an unusual golden-brown colour is produced with milk containing nitrates when the butyrometer is shaken. The colour is different from the gradual production of the purplish-brown coloration obtained with pure milk.

A more sensitive method exists for nitrate in which a mercury reagent is added to milk, the mixture is filtered after vigorous shaking and diphenylamine is added. The presence of nitrates gives a dark-blue coloration.

The above methods are not, however, reliable in terms of showing the presence of extraneous water and are at best qualitative and insensitive. The method most widely used is the freezing point test.

5.3 Freezing point test for detecting adulteration

5.3.1 Basis of the test

The osmotic pressure, or salt balance, of a cow's milk has to be in balance with that of her blood. Since the osmotic pressure of a cow's blood can only vary within narrow limits it follows that the salt balance of her milk—and hence the freezing point, dictated by salt balance—can only vary within narrow limits.

5.3.2   *Freezing point depression and how it is controlled*

Pure water freezes at 0°C. However, when solutes are added to water the freezing point is depressed. This explains why seawater, containing dissolved salts, freezes at about −1 or −2°C and why salt is added to roads in the winter—to depress the freezing point. Similarly, the solutes (lactose, dissolved salts, etc.) in milk depress its freezing point.

Hence, the average freezing point of normal milk is about 0.5°C below the freezing point of water. The cow maintains a balance between the osmotic pressure of her milk and that of her blood by addition of saline solutions to milk. In cows with acute mastitis, for example, where the lactose level is depressed, the cow compensates by lifting the osmotic pressure by adding a little salt. This is why acute mastitic milk tastes salty.

5.3.3   *Measurement units*

The original work on freezing points was undertaken by Hortvet who used a mercury in glass thermometer. More recent works show that Hortvet's measurements were slightly inaccurate. However, since much of the early recorded data are based on measurements in Hortvet's apparatus some countries still calibrate according to the Hortvet scale whereas others use the true Celcius scale. It is possible to correct results from one method to another using the following formulae:

$$°C = 0.96418°H + 0.00085$$
$$°H = 1.03711°C - 0.00085$$

The two scales differ in bias and slope with 0.540°H (°C measured by Hortvet) equating to 0.521°C true Celcius. The data given in this text is based on Hortvet measurements and for the sake of convenience will be referred to as °H.

5.3.4   *How constant is the freezing point of milk?*

Data have been gathered from many countries to establish the true variation in the freezing point of milk. There is little difference between countries or between breed of cow, or between seasons. The distribution of herd freezing points fits a bell-shaped curve (Figure 5.1). The average freezing point of genuine milk is −0.543°H, i.e. the freezing point of water is depressed by a little over 0.5°H.

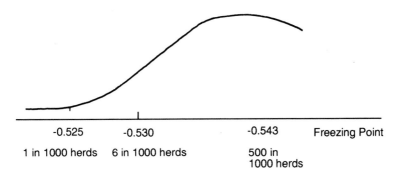

| -0.525 | -0.530 | -0.543 | Freezing Point |
| 1 in 1000 herds | 6 in 1000 herds | 500 in 1000 herds | |

Figure 5.1 Distribution of herd freezing points.

There is a small number of herds (about 6 in a 1000) where the freezing point depression (FDP) of the milk is less than 0.530°H, and it is virtually unknown for herd milk, providing it is free from extraneous water, to have a FPD as low as −0.525°H.

The difference between the average FPD of all herds (0.543°H) and that for a single herd of say 0.530°H is equivalent to about 2.5% 'added' water. Herein lies the dilemma for the prosecuting authorities which have to strike a balance between protecting the consumer and ensuring that the honest farmers, who supply milk with *genuinely* low freezing points, are not unfairly penalised. The balance struck is as follows:

- Where the FPD is greater than −0.535°H the supply is assumed to be free from extraneous water. (Even though compared with an average supply this could have up to 1% extraneous water at this FPD.)
- Where the freezing point is between −0.530 and −0.534°H a letter is sent to the producer advising him/her to check their plant.
- Where a supply is −0.525 to −0.529°H there is a strong probability that extraneous water is present. If there is real doubt about the possibility of extraneous water, 'appeal to the herd' testing is recommended to establish the genuine FPD of the milk in question to compare it with suspect samples.
- Where the freezing point depression is −0.525°H or less, it is assumed that the supply contains extraneous water, and the onus of proof of innocence is put on the farmer (Figure 5.2).

5.3.5 Freezing point of goat's, buffalo's and ewe's milk

The freezing point of goat's milk, buffalo's milk and ewe's milk have all been reported in the literature (chapter 7).

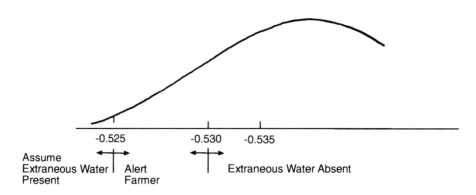

Figure 5.2   Action to be taken on freezing point results.

The general conclusions are that the freezing points of goat's and ewe's milk are generally slightly lower than cow's milk and that buffalo's milk has a freezing point similar to cow's milk.

5.3.6   Factors affecting the freezing point of milk

The factors affecting the freezing point of milk have been fully reviewed in IDF (1983).

There are a few millidegrees difference in the freezing points of milk from different breeds of cows but there is little significant lactational effect. The greatest impact on freezing point of genuine milk is abnormal water intake by the cow. The freezing point can be abnormally elevated ($-0.500°$H and above) if a herd is deprived of water for some time then given ad lib access prior to milking. Very bad feeding can also give elevated freezing points.

Care should be taken to test only fresh samples since conversion of each molecule of lactose to four molecules of lactic acid (Figure 4.4) will actually depress the freezing point such that the presence of extraneous water could be masked. Samples should therefore be transported for freezing point tests under refrigeration conditions. Where this is not practicable a preservative may be used to prevent bacterial spoilage. Results on preserved samples must however be treated with great caution.

It is normal to test for titratable acidity at the same time as completing the freezing point test to ensure that developed acidity is not influencing the measurement and masking the confirmation of adulteration.

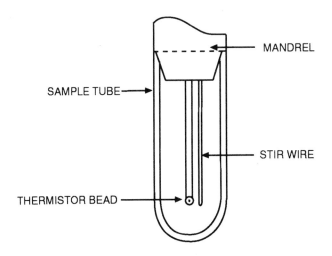

Figure 5.3 Cryoscope sample tube with stirrer and thermistor head.

5.3.7 Test method

The test method currently involves measurement of the freezing point by means of a thermistor cryoscope. A 2 ml sample of milk is held in a sample tube immersed in a bath at −7°C. The temperature of the sample is measured using a thermistor, centred in the body of the sample which is stirred by a vibrating stirrer wire (Figure 5.3).

Initially, the sample is supercooled to about −3°C, ice crystals are formed by a pulse of energy causing the stirrer wire to strike the walls of the tube giving a 'freeze pulse'. Latent heat of fusion is released as the super-cooled milk changes to ice and the sample temperature rises to a freezing point plateau (Figure 5.4) at which the freezing point is measured.

5.3.8 Calculation of amount of extraneous water in milk

The principle of the calculation is that pure water freezes at 0°C and pure milk freezes at (say) −0.540°H. Therefore, assuming a linear relationship, each 1% extraneous water will move the freezing point of the mixture 1/100th of the difference, i.e. 0.0054°H closer to 0°C (Figure 5.5).

This calculation assumes an average value for genuine milk.

The calculation used is

$$W = \frac{(C - D)(100 - S)}{C}$$

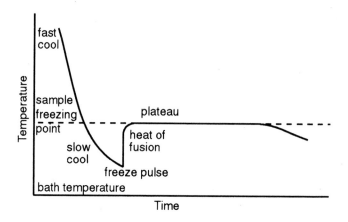

Figure 5.4   Freezing point plateau of milk.

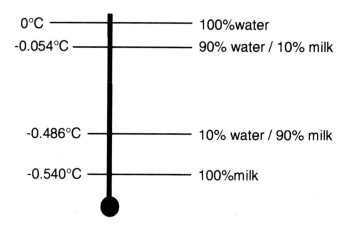

Figure 5.5   Calculation of the percentage water in milk from the freezing point test.

where W is the % (m/m) of extraneous water in the milk, C is the actual, or assumed reference freezing point of genuine milk, D is the measured freezing point of the suspect milk, and S is the % (m/m) of total solids of the suspect milk.

If there is a real doubt about the genuine freezing point of herd milk to be used as a reference point against which to judge a suspect case of extraneous water, an 'appeal to the cow' or genuine authenticated sample should be taken within 48 h of the suspect test. The authenticated sample involves sampling the milk from the suspect herd under supervised conditions. Supervisors should ensure that no extraneous water finds access during milking and that all pipes, etc. are thoroughly drained. It may be desirable to flush the pipework through with the first few litres of milk which will be kept out of the authentic sample.

5.4 Sources of contamination by extraneous water

Although purposeful adulteration of milk with water is believed to be rare, milk production and processing plants are 'wet cleaned' and sterilised, hence it is virtually impossible to eliminate totally the ingress of small quantities of extraneous water. An essential starting point is an installation designed to allow adequate drainage. In some production plants a sponge plug can be forced through the plant to squeeze out traces of trapped water. In processing plants the 'first milk through' should be segregated and checked for extraneous water before being sold.

Attempts have been made to quantify the water likely to be present in well drained milking installations. In one investigation the milking plant was drained as completely as possible before milking yet a change in the freezing point of the milk corresponding to 0.5% added water was still noted when 12 cows were milked, or 0.4% when 24 cows were milked.

It has been suggested that the presence of detergent/sterilisers might mask the presence of extraneous water. However, a mixture of at least 2% of these solutions is needed to compensate for the effect of the added water. Such a concentration is not likely to be encountered in practice and residues at this level would be likely to taint the milk.

Water trapped in milking plants can influence the freezing point of milk. Efficient drainage of the milking plant is therefore of the greatest importance. It is also important to prevent ingress of extraneous water from condensation or leaking coolers. Sources of extraneous water are

(a) inadequate draining of plant before milking,
(b) a leaking cooler or water valve,
(c) careless dipping of clusters between milking cows,
(d) 'sweeping through' the pipeline with water at the end of milking, and
(e) accidentally switching on the automatic cleaning system before the bulk vat is emptied or the pipeline diverted.

5.5 How to avoid getting water into milk at the farm

For churn or can collected milk, cans and surface coolers should be checked to ensure that they do not leak. For parlour milking systems the following precautions should be observed:

- *Before milking*
    (a) Drain all parts of the pipeline, the recorder jar, milk pump, clusters, bulk vat, buckets and churns (if used).
    (b) If possible, avoid having a water supply connected directly to the milk line, with a single isolation valve. If such a system is used, check the valve for water seepage when under vacuum.
    (c) If a 'back-flushing' system is used for rinsing the clusters, make sure that the valve is functioning correctly (check under vacuum) so that water does not enter the milk-line.

- *During milking*
    (a) Dry cow's udders thoroughly after washing, using a fresh paper towel.
    (b) If clusters are 'dipped' in a sterilising solution between cows, shake the clusters well in order to remove excess water.

- *After milking*
    (a) Drain all milk from the pipeline, receiver jar and milk pump into a clean bucket. Do not flush this milk through to the bulk vat with water.
    (b) Divert the pipeline from the bulk vat before rinsing the milking plant to waste.
    (c) Make sure that the bulk vat cleaning system cannot be switched on accidentally while there is milk in the vat.

A simple method which can be used by field staff on the farm for measuring the amount of extraneous water residing in milking equipment involves weighing 15.5 litres of tap water in a bucket, dissolving in it 750 g of salt and measuring its density. The solution is then passed five times through the plant and the density is measured again. The difference in density is used as a measure of the residual water in the plant and the method is said to be accurate to 0.6 litres of residual water.

5.6 Control of extraneous water through payment schemes

The freezing point test offers a sound means of measuring and quantifying the amount of extraneous water in milk and is widely used as a rejection test and in prosecution cases. However, a good disincentive for extraneous water is to pay farmers on kg fat and protein; this then gives no benefit to farmers adding water. The disincentive can be heightened by using a negative payment related to the volume being collected. However, since even with payment schemes not every consignment is sampled and tested, the freezing point test will continue to be used as a means of controlling extraneous water.

5.7 Other sources of adulteration

Whenever there is a control system there is always the possibility that someone will try to find a way around it. Occasions have occurred where milk has been adulterated with sugar, salt or even milk powder in order to 'lift' the freezing point, masking the addition of extraneous water or to elevate the SNF of milk.

5.7.1 Salt

The addition of salt (sodium chloride) solutions will have little effect on the total solids or SNF of milk but the salt will significantly elevate the FPD hence masking the measurement of extraneous water. However, salt is readily detected in milk. Salty milk is obvious from its taste and since the chloride content of milk is quite low (14% of ash or 0.09% of milk) added levels can also be easily measured.

The measurement involves ashing milk, after which the chloride can be titrated against standard silver nitrate using potassium chromate as an indicator. Measurement may also be made directly on milk or cream where 9ml is transferred into a porcelain dish, 1ml of potassium dichromate is added and the chloride is titrated against 0.1M silver nitrate to the first of a pale-red colour.

$$\% \text{ chloride} = \frac{\text{ml of } 0.1\text{M silver nitrate} \times 3.55}{\text{weight of sample}}$$

5.7.2 Sugar

Like salt, sugar may be added to mask addition of extraneous water. Sugar will impart an uncharacteristically sweet taste to milk. Its presence can be detected down to about 0.05% by using the following test: 2 ml of a saturated solution of ammonium molybdate and 8 ml of hydrochloric acid are added to 10 ml of milk. The temperature of the mixture is raised gradually to 80°C (not above) for 5 min, when a blue colour is formed if sucrose (cane sugar) is present.

5.7.3   Skim-milk powder

Its use as an adulterant is most unusual primarily because it is not cost-effective for the farmer to add milk powder. If used, powders will normally result in deposits being obvious in the bottom of churns or bulk vats. Test methods are available and are based on the identification of heat denatured products in milk powders.

5.7.4   Detergent sterilants

Detergents/sterilants are usually only found in milk as a result of accidental addition of cleaning agents. This is usually easily detected by the extraneous water test, as the detergent itself does not significantly effect the freezing point. Strong detergents usually impart an odd odour and taste to the milk.

5.7.5   Preservatives

If milk is of dubious microbiological quality there might be a temptation to use an antimicrobial agent to act as a preservative. Their use is usually prohibited by law. Substances which have been used include boric acid, formaldehyde, hydrogen peroxide, hypochlorite etc. and there are many 'spot' tests for these preservatives.

5.7.5.1   Boric acid and borates.   Boric acid and borates are readily detected in milk by placing a few drops of the milk sample in a depression on a spot plate, adding a few drops of turmeric tincture and 2 drops of hydrochloric acid. After mixing the solution with a glass rod the tile is warmed on a waterbath until the milk is dry. If boric acid is present a pink colour will develop—which changes to olive green if sodium bicarbonate solution is added. The test detects 0.005% boric acid in milk.

5.7.5.2   Formaldehyde.   Formaldehyde is obvious in milk as during the Gerber test it gives rise to a deep purple colour. Very low levels are also demonstrated when a little milk is heated with three to five times its volume of concentrated hydrochloric acid (which must have a trace of boric chloride).

Schiff's reagent may also be used as a confirmatory test. A little of the suspect milk is curdled with dilute sulphuric acid and a little Schiff's reagent (a solution of rosaniline bleached by sulphurous acid) is added to the filtrate in a test tube. The tube is cooled and a violet-pink colour is produced if formaldehyde is present.

5.7.5.3 Hydrogen peroxide. Werther's test consists of adding 10 drops of a 1% solution of sodium orthovanadate in 10% sulphuric acid to 10 ml of milk; the presence of hydrogen peroxide gives rise to a red coloration.

5.7.5.4 Hypochlorite. Since hypochlorites are the most commonly used sterilising agents they are the most likely preservative to be found in milk. As the presence of chlorine may be transient it is usual to test for chlorate, which is present in all hypochlorite solutions and can be detected at least 4 days after the hypochlorite addition with no loss of sensitivity. The test involves cooling 3 ml of milk in a test tube to 0–5°C. Three millilitres of 73.5% sulphuric acid containing 0.025% stannous chloride (at 0–5°C) are added and the contents of the tube are shaken in a cooling mixture of ice and salt. The tube is allowed to stand for 3 min and the contents are transferred to a centrifuge tube and spun at 2500 rpm for 3 min. The tube is then examined in ultraviolet light for a yellow fluoresence.

If any of the above spot tests for preservatives are to be used it is recommended that samples spiked with preservatives and blank samples are also tested to confirm the test regime.

5.7.6 Colostrum

Where block calving is common, as in New Zealand, early season milk can contain high levels of colostrum. Colostrum is the milk secreted by the cow during the first 3 days after parturition. Colostrum has almost double the total solids of ordinary milk. However, it has a very high proportion of the protein immunoglobulin and this can give rise to manufacturing problems.

5.7.6.1 Manufacturing problems associated with colostrum. Immunoglobulins readily denature on heating causing 'burn on' in evaporators and on heat exchangers in pasteurisation plants. This protein deposit reduces heat transfer and significantly increases cleaning costs.

Product faults may also be a result of high levels of colostrum in milk. Concentrated milk and evaporated milk can be unstable and graininess develops if the milk used in its manufacture contains too much colostrum. Colostrum can also impart colour and flavour defects in butter and milk powders.

In countries where block calving is practised and these production faults are evident therefore, testing for colostrum is regularly undertaken.

5.7.6.2 Test methods. Attempts have been made to qualitatively assess colostrum levels by colour or consistency of milk but these tests are not sufficiently discriminating. Tests designed for mastitis have been used with limited success. Heat stability tests and the alcohol stability test are time consuming and not very discriminating.

A test kit, suitable for on-farm and laboratory use, is now available. In the test, milk is pipetted into wells in an agar plate containing an immunoglobulin antiserum. Any immunoglobulin in the milk diffuses into the agar to form a precipitation zone around the well and the size of the zone is compared with standards and with a standard graph. Standards are used on each test plate. The test takes 24 h to perform. Penalties are often levied if milk tests at 0.2% or greater. Testing is only necessary for the first two months of a season with block calving herds.

5.7.6.3 Action to be taken by farmers. Milk from freshly calved cows should be kept out of the milk being sold for 4 days after calving. Colostrum, being rich in protein and high in immune proteins to protect the young calf, is valuable and should be used for stock feed.

5.7.7 Blood

Blood finds access to milk from damaged udders.The presence of blood in milk is undesirable for aesthetic reasons since its presence would be unacceptable to consumers and because blood is likely to carry with it bacteria and enzymes which may affect the quality of milk. For these reasons a processor has the right to reject milk which contains blood.

The level at which it is reasonable to reject milk is not precisely set. However, test methods have been standardised to ensure equity. A standardised test means that all laboratories are able to judge milk samples against a common test method and set an agreed rejection standard.

The most commonly used test is the centrifuge test in which 10 ml of milk, warmed to 65°C, is centrifuged under standard conditions. The blood, being more dense than milk, deposits in the test tube under centrifugation and is compared with photographic standards prepared from additions of standard volumes of blood (0–100ppm) to milk. As milk ages any blood cells present tend to lyse giving rise to detection of lower apparent levels. Blood tests should therefore be made on fresh milk otherwise false negatives may result.

Red test tube deposits can be confirmed as being blood by the use of clinical strips such as Hemastix reagent strips—or Gum Guaiac which are used in human clinical chemistry.

Soluble blood can also be determined in milk by measuring the absorbance at 396 nm after treatment with acetic acid. The method requires preparation of a standard curve using known concentrations of blood in milk.

Farmers should keep individual cow milks containing blood out of the herd bulk milk supply. Blood is sometimes present in milk during the first few days after calving or can find access through damage to the teat.

Teats should be inspected for cuts or abrasions prior to milking and any milk showing visual signs of blood should be kept out of the bulked supply and should be used for stockfeed.

5.7.8 Taints

There are a wide range of potential taints in milk—many of which arise through feedingstuffs. Sugar beet, for example, can give rise to fishy taints and some weeds to garlic taints or malty taints. Some of these taints are removed in the processing of milk. However, farmers are wise to maintain a check on the milk they supply in order to minimise the risk of taints which may result in their milk being rejected.

A more permanent and potentially devastating taint can arise from disinfectants. Phenolic chemicals are widely used in domestic drain disinfectants, udder salves or fly sprays and cresols, chemicals of the phenol family, which are used in wood preservatives such as creosote. These chemicals by themselves are a potential source of taints at the ppm level, however when they react with free chlorine, which can arise from the widely used sterilising agent hypochlorite, they form chlorophenols. The family of chlorophenols cause taints in milk at levels as low as one part per billion parts of milk. Chlorophenols are not easily detected by smell, hence may not be noticed by the tanker driver at the time of collecting the milk. They do however make milk unpalatable to the consumer at very low concentrations (1 ppb) hence one farmer's supply could contaminate a silo or even a production run for which he may be held financially accountable. When this occurs the farmers responsible may have to pay for large volumes of wasted milk. Great care is needed in checking the type of chemicals used in the milking parlour, since phenolic materials can be present in udder salves and creams, drain cleaners/disinfectants or fly sprays.

Farmers should only use approved disinfectants if they are to avoid the problem of taints in milk and processors should check all incoming tankers before off-loading. Control for taints involves the processor arranging for milk to be routinely tasted. Surprisingly this is still the most sensitive overall control method. Samples should be laboratory pasteurised then tasted by either an individual laboratory assistant, known to be sensitive to the taint based on tasting trials using spiked samples, or preferably by a taste panel comprising five people screened in tasting.

References and further reading

Binder, W. (1970) Preservation of milk samples intended for freezing point determination. *Food Sci. Technol. Abstr.*, **2**(1), 110 (Abstr. 1, p. 70).

BSI (1988) *Recommendations for the Interpretation of the Freezing Point of Herd Milk* (BS 3095: Part 2). British Standards Institute, London, UK.

Coveney, L. (1993) The freezing point depression of authenticated and bulk vat milk. Results of surveys 1989–91. *J. Soc. Dairy Technol.*, **46**(2), 43–46.

IDF (1983) Measurement of extraneous water by the freezing point tests. (Document 154). IDF, Brussels, Belgium.

6 Compositional quality

F. HARDING

6.1 Composition of milk

Mammals secrete milk to supply nutrition to their young. For centuries man has taken advantage of this by taking milk from cows, water buffaloes, goats and sheep (450–500 million metric tons per year worldwide) and using it to make a significant contribution to his diet.

The composition of milk from different mammals varies enormously. In order to provide high energy to their offspring, whales and porpoises produce milk with a fat content in excess of 40%, elephants produce milk of about 20% fat and reindeer, milk of over 15% fat. Cows, like humans, produce milk of a lower fat content—close to 4%.

Cows produce more milk than their offspring require and man has taken advantage of this since the dawn of time. Breeding programmes have successfully increased the amount and quality of milk cows produce. Cow's milk contains about 87.4% water and about 12.6% milk solids (total solids) the latter comprising about 3.9% fat, 3.2% protein, 4.6% lactose (anhydrous) and 0.9% 'other solids', i.e. minerals, vitamins, etc. (Figure 6.1). Non-water constituents are present in different physical forms; dissolved (lactose), colloidally dispersed (protein) and emulsified in water (lipids or fats). These physical characteristics are used to facilitate the commercial and analytical separation of the major constituents of milk.

6.2 Measurement of total solids in milk

The 'total solids' of milk are determined simply by evaporating the water and weighing the residue. For the reference method the conditions for the measurement are tightly controlled and rely on oven drying 5 g of milk at $102 \pm 1°C$ for 2 h until constant mass is achieved. These methods are detailed in IDF, AOAC and ISO standards. Care has to be taken in keeping the solids matter in a dry atmosphere (desiccator) whilst it is being cooled prior to weighing, since lactose is extremely hygroscopic and will readily pick up water, thus giving a falsely high total solids figure. For products such as yogurts and cultured milks, which contain volatile acids, neutralisation with sodium hydroxide or zinc oxide is necessary in order to bind and hence prevent loss of these acids during drying. The

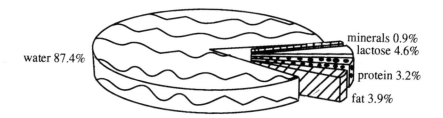

Figure 6.1   Gross composition of milk.

weight of the added neutraliser is taken into account in the final weighing process.

Moisture balances have been used for rapid determination of total solids. These consist of a combined balance and radiant infrared drying lamp. Whilst these may be used for measuring total solids of milk they tend to be used more for measuring moisture (water) in milk products.

Similarly microwave ovens have been used for the rapid determination of total solids in milk. These routine drying methods have to be checked regularly against the reference method in order to establish a calibration control.

Mechanised pipetting followed by oven drying in a flow-through tunnel leading to a balance have in the past been used for mass testing for total solids where it has been used for quality payment of farmers. However, milk total solids is now considered to be a very crude measure of quality and most payment systems are based on fat and solids-not-fat or fat and protein.

Milk total solids (TS) comprise fat (3.9%) and solids-not-fat (8.7%) (SNF), sometimes referred to as non-fat milk solids (NFMS).

6.3   Measurement of the solids-not-fat (SNF) of milk

SNF by definition are the total solids other than butterfat. The reference SNF therefore is obtained by taking the reference oven-drying total solids and subtracting the reference (solvent extraction) butterfat.

$$SNF = TS - FAT$$

Many retail products such as creams, butter, etc. are manufactured from fat separated from milk, hence creating a different commercial value for fat than for SNF. As some countries have made SNF a payment parameter for farmers, more rapid, less labour-intensive measurement systems than the reference method have been sought.

(a)

Figure 6.2 Hydrometer for measuring solids-not-fat in milk.

Mechanical oven-drying total solids and mechanised Gerber fat determination systems have been used to provide TS and fat—hence SNF.

Measurement of the density of milk using a hydrometer or lactometer
(Figure 6.2) together with determination of fat by Gerber has also been
used for routine measurement of fat and SNF. This method gives a simple
approximation to the gravimetric SNF. The method is based on the different specific gravities of fat (0.93) water (1.0) and SNF (1.6) of milk. It
is based on the observation that the density of milk at a standard temperature (20°C) is related to the fat and SNF content. Hence, measurement of fat (Gerber) and density enables the SNF to be calculated.

The following formula was arrived at by measuring gravimetric SNF,
density and fat for thousands of herd milk samples

$$TS = 0.25D + 1.22 \text{ fat} + 0.72SNF$$
$$SNF = TS - \text{fat}$$

where TS is total solids and D is density (at 20°C). This derived formula
for SNF gives an approximate SNF for individual milk supplies.

It is important that errors in density determination are minimised by
use of calibrated hydrometers and thermometers. However, the density
method of measuring SNF is at best an approximation to the more accurate reference gravimetric method.

Infrared instruments measuring fat, protein and lactose can also provide an SNF or total solids figure when suitable allowances are made for the 'other constituents' or 'mineral bias' of milk since the SNF (8.7%) in turn is composed of protein (3.2%), and lactose or milk sugar (4.6%) with vitamins and minerals adding a further 0.9%. The accuracy of such an SNF estimate will depend upon accurate calibration of the infrared instrument for protein and lactose, and regular checks of the constant to be applied for 'other constituents'. This is obtained from measurement of gravimetric SNF, from which reference protein and lactose is subtracted. The 0.92% 'value' proposed for 'other solids' is an average and will vary slightly from herd to herd.

The composition of cow's milk varies from cow to cow within breeds, and from breed to breed. It also varies during a lactation, seasonally and regionally and there are many factors which cause these variations. Milk composition is important since the yields of products made from milk depend on the quantity of particular constituents present in the raw milk (see chapter 8). Since the cost of the raw material, milk, accounts for about 70% of the cost of products, the financial value of each litre of milk is directly related to its compositional quality, hence it would be illogical to pay farmers only on the volume they sell. In most countries therefore compositional quality is one of the factors used to calculate the payment to farmers.

6.4   Major constituents

6.4.1   Fat

The lipids or fats of milk cumulatively are referred to as butterfat. Biologically, due to the high percentage of carbon in fats, they are 'stored' nutrients with the highest energy or calorific value of all food constituents. The basic structure involves esterification of fatty acids onto a glycerol molecule (Figure 6.3).

R, R' and R'' represent fatty acids which may be the same, or different. Fatty acids are organic acids composed of hydrocarbon chains with a carboxyl group (–COOH) on one end. These can be short-chain, long-chain, saturated or unsaturated.

Saturated fatty acids have no double bonds, monounsaturated one and polyunsaturated two or more double bonds. In oils from fish or plants, fatty acids tend to be polyunsaturated (PUFA) whereas animal fats tend to be saturated. However, the fatty acids of butterfat vary in chain length and in levels of monounsaturates and this variation can affect both the nutritional value of fat and the quality and characteristics of products made from it. Milk fat contains more short-chain fatty acids (C_4 and C_6)

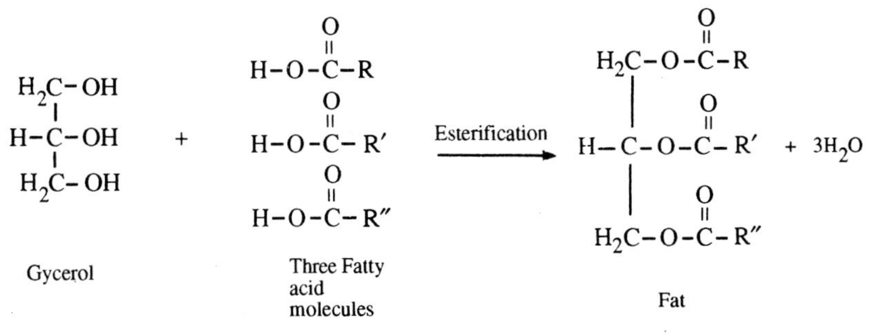

Figure 6.3 Structure of fat molecule.

than most vegetable oils. The major fatty acids in milk are given in Table 6.1.

6.4.1.1 Measurement of fat: quantity. The fat content and its type are of considerable commercial and nutritional importance to the dairy industry. The measurement of fat has therefore been the preoccupation of dairy chemists since the 1800s.

The earliest methods of measuring fat content were solvent extraction techniques in which, after initial digestion of a known weight of the sample to liberate the fat, fat is extracted by solvents which are subsequently evaporated. The extracted fat is weighed and the fat content of the milk can then be calculated using the following formula:

$$\frac{\text{weight of fat extracted}}{\text{weight of milk taken}} \times 100 = \text{butterfat \%}$$

These gravimetric methods are still used as reference methods of measuring fat, and milk fat by definition is that which is extractable by these methods. The reference method used for measuring fat in milk is the Rose–Gottlieb method in which alcohol and ammonia are added to 10 g of milk. The alcohol causes the protein to precipitate and free the fat. The ammonia dissolves the protein and the fat is then extracted into diethyl ether and petroleum ether. The separated solvent is evaporated and the dried butterfat is weighed. This method is used to determine fat in milk and a number of milk products. Tougher digestion systems using hydrochloric acid (Schmid–Bondzynski–Ratzlaff and Weibull–Berntrop) are required for some milk products and for milk-based foods such as custards which contain non-milk ingredients.

These solvent extraction techniques are time-consuming and expensive to operate hence more rapid methods have been sought for routine

Table 6.1 Major fatty acids in milk[a]

	Number of carbon atoms: number of double bonds	Approx. content (% weight)
Saturated		
Butyric	4:0	2.8
Caproic	6:0	2.3
Caprylic	8:0	1.1
Capric	10:0	3.0
Lauric	12:0	2.9
Myristic	14:0	8.9
Palmitic	16:0	24
Stearic	18:0	13.2
Unsaturated		
Myristoleic	14:1	0.7
Palmitoleic	16:1	1.8
Oleic	18:1	29.6
Linoleic	18:2	2.1
Linolenic	18:3	0.5

[a]Source: Campbell and Marshall (1975).

testing. Butyrometric methods were initially developed to meet the criteria of speed and economy. There are a number of varieties of butyrometric determinations of fat but the principle of the methods is the same and they can be used for measuring the fat content not only of milk but also of milk products.

In the Gerber method a standard volume of milk (10.94 ml in the UK) is pipetted and treated with sulphuric acid and amyl alcohol in a specially calibrated tube called a butyrometer (Figure 6.4). Mixing of the strong sulphuric acid and water from milk creates heat which helps digest the milk protein in the sample. The liberation of the fat is assisted by amyl alcohol and the tube is then centrifuged under standard conditions. After equilibration in a water bath at 65°C the fat content of the sample is read directly from the calibrated part of the butyrometer. The Babcock test is another butyrometric technique and is widely used in the USA.

Attempts to use various alkaline reagents to replace sulphuric acid, for safety and convenience, have failed to give the same efficient digestion as sulphuric acid hence such alternative systems are rarely used.

Fat testing therefore has had two historic periods: the development of gravimetric methods which are still used as the reference test methods, and the development of routine butyrometric methods. The latter were widely used for routine quality control of milk through from the early 1900s until the late 1960s. Butyrometric testing was also used in early mass testing laboratories where large numbers of samples had to be tested for dairy herd improvement or quality payment testing.

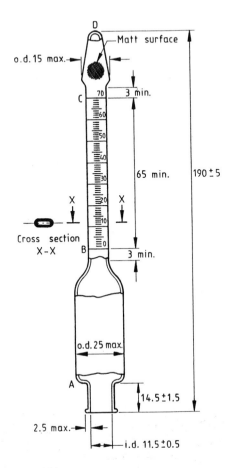

Figure 6.4 Milk fat butyrometer. By courtesy of the British Standards Institution.

This application however was far from ideal as even with automatic dispensing of sulphuric acid and amyl alcohol, laboratory working conditions were hazardous and would hardly have met modern legal requirements for safety at work. In addition, the massive task of disposing of vast volumes of sulphuric acid required sodium carbonate neutralisation pits and even then gave major problems in terms of drain deterioration and effluent disposal.

It was not surprising therefore that a third generation of fat testing came to the fore. This third generation was instrumental analysis which first saw the light in the early 1960's. Instrumental methods are now widely used as manual, semiautomatic, automatic and even on-line versions and these are discussed later. Instrumental methods however need to be calibrated and standards for instrument calibration are still obtained by use of reference methods such as the Rose–Gottlieb or Gerber methods.

6.4.1.2 Quality: Adulteration of the fat in milk. There are many fats cheaper than butterfat, hence methods have been sought to establish that the fat measured in milk is truly butterfat and not a poorer substitute. Methods for differentiating butterfat from other fats rely on the fact that butterfat contains a significant proportion of low-molecular-weight steam volatile acids which are soluble in water. This was the basis of early work on the purity of butterfat.

A number of early analysts worked on techniques for establishing the purity of butterfat culminating in the Reichert–Polenske–Kirschner technique. This technique involves extraction of butterfat (about 20 g) from milk and titration of the soluble fatty acids which distil over with steam under carefully specified conditions (Reichert). The Polenske, insoluble volatile acid, value is obtained by titration of the alcoholic solution of the insoluble volatile acids. The Kirschner value depends on the solubility of silver butyrate in dilute silver nitrate solution whilst the silver salts of higher fatty acids are practically insoluble.

Genuine butterfat usually gives Reichert values between 24 and 33 and in routine examinations it is usually sufficient to carry out only a Reichert determination. If a value of over 24 is obtained it is unnecessary to carry out the Polenske or Kirschner determinations.

More modern techniques involve comparing the fatty acid profile of milk, measured by gas chromatography, with values in the literature (chapter 7).

6.4.2 Proteins

Proteins are the most valuable components of milk in terms of their importance in human nutrition and their influence on the properties of dairy products containing them. This, together with the availability of rapid instrumental methods of measurement, has led to increased use of protein as a quality parameter in payment of farmers.

Proteins are large-molecular-weight complex organic compounds which contain carbon, hydrogen, oxygen and nitrogen; sulphur, phosphorus and other elements may also be present. Protein molecules are made up of amino acids. These link together via peptide bonds to form long chains (Figure 6.5).

The variety of proteins which can be produced from the wide variety of amino acid building blocks, together with variations possible in the number of units in the chain, is extremely large and makes the study of proteins complex.

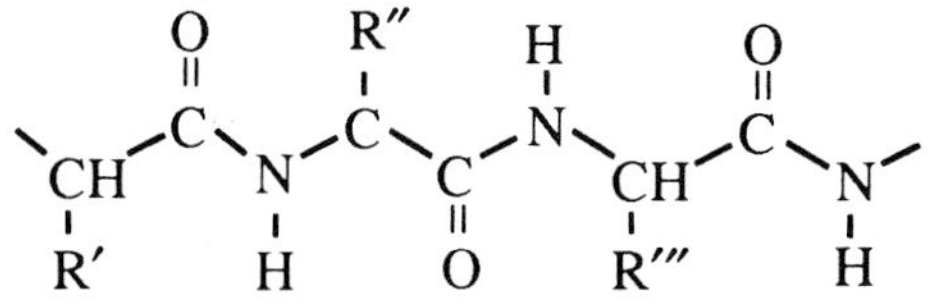

Figure 6.5 Structure of protein molecule, having three component amino acids.

6.4.2.1 Measurement of protein. A common factor in all proteins is the presence of nitrogen in reasonably constant proportions and this led to nineteenth century Danish chemist Kjeldahl, then working for Carlsberg breweries, to develop what has become the classical reference method for determination of protein. The method is a tribute to the technical skills of the analysts of that time since it has stood the test of time and is still used as *the* reference method for determining the protein content of most foodstuffs.

The Kjeldahl method involves digesting 10 g of milk with strong sulphuric acid and potassium sulphate (used to raise the temperature during digestion) in the presence of a catalyst such as cupric sulphate. Organic matter is oxidised during the digestion and nitrogen is quantitatively converted to ammonium sulphate.

After digestion is complete, and the contents have been cooled, the digest is made alkaline by addition of concentrated sodium hydroxide solution. The ammonia formed in the digestion step is thus released from protein nitrogen, distilled into boric acid or a standard acid and determined by titration.

This then gives a measure of the nitrogen content of the sample from which a 'total' or 'crude' protein content is calculated. In arriving at the conversion factor for nitrogen to protein, Kjeldahl noted that nitrogen represented about 16% by weight of average protein. He calculated therefore that by multiplying the nitrogen measured by a factor of 100/16, i.e. about 6.25 (6.38 for milk) one could express nitrogen, determined by his techniques, as protein.

Our knowledge about the wide range of proteins found in milk has increased dramatically in recent years. It is a credit to Kjeldahl that even with this knowledge current calculations still confirm his findings.

There are other test methods which can be used to measure protein in milk. Instrumental methods involving dye binding or infrared are described later, these secondary methods however still need to be calibrated against the reference Kjeldahl method.

Although there are a large number of different nitrogenous compounds in milk as determined by the Kjeldahl method, these tend to be grouped in three broad categories: caseins, whey proteins and non-protein nitrogen (NPN). This classification was formalised by Rowland who crudely fractionated proteins in milk by acid precipitation and measured the Kjeldahl nitrogen content of each of the fractions.

Rowlands technique involves three Kjeldahl measurements. The first is the determination of the total nitrogen content by Kjeldahl. The second involves precipitation of true protein using 12% trichloroacetic acid and measurement of Kjeldahl nitrogen of the precipitate to give a direct measure of the true protein. Alternatively the nitrogen content of the filtrate can be measured in order to provide NPN, results from which true protein can then be calculated.

$$\text{Total protein} - \text{NPN} = \text{true protein}$$

In the Rowlands method casein is precipitated from milk using acetic acid and sodium acetate and nitrogen is determined on the filtrate. These methods have been widely studied and are used in International standard methods for measuring the protein fractions of milk.

Studies of large numbers of bulk samples showed that about 76% of total protein is represented by casein, 18% by whey proteins and 6% by NPN (Table 6.2). The casein fraction of milk is of especial commercial importance since caseins are captured in cheesemaking whereas whey proteins and NPN are lost to the whey. Because of their desirable functional properties whey proteins have become of commercial interest and may be extracted from whey by ultrafiltration.

The NPN fraction consists of low molecular weight nitrogenous material not precipitated by 12% trichloracetic acid in the Rowlands method. About half of the NPN in milk is accounted for by urea.

For quality payment purposes most countries use total (crude) protein (total Kjeldahl nitrogen × 6.38) as the reference base, although France, a major cheesemaking country, uses 'true' protein by discounting NPN (Kjeldahl total N − NPN) when calibrating quality payment testing instruments. This in effect leads to a protein base some 6% lower than would occur if total protein were used.

6.4.2.2 The future. In view of the dangers inherent in the Kjeldahl method it is likely to be replaced in time by the Dumas method.

Different milk proteins have different impacts on cheese yield and cheesemaking properties. κ-casein BB is believed to enhance cheesemaking and selection of bulls of enhanced genetic merit is now becoming possible by analysis of semen. Further research is now under way to examine the relationship between milk protein genotypes, milk production traits and milk processing characteristics. This work is likely to be the start of detailed genetic selection for enhanced milk quality characteristics which,

Table 6.2 Protein fractions in milk

	As a percentage of	
	Milk	Total protein
True protein (TP–NPN)	3.06	94
Casein	2.48	76.3
Whey proteins	0.58	17.9
NPN	0.18	5.8
Total (crude) protein (TP)	3.25	100

[a]Source: Harding and Royal (1974b).

if linked with multiple production (cloning), could lead to the future tailoring of milk to meet specific desirable processing characteristics.

6.4.3 Lactose

Lactose, with the exception of water, is, at about 4.6%, the principal component of milk yet it is the least important of the solids both nutritionally and commercially. Lactose—milk sugar—is the major carbohydrate in the milk of most mammals. Hence mammalian milk is the major source of lactose, one of the most common natural disaccharides. Lactose consists of two molecules, D-glucose and D-galactose (Figure 6.6) and is digested or broken down into these constituent parts by the enzyme lactase.

Lactose plays a major role in the characteristics of condensed milk products. It also supplies the carbohydrate sources for bacterial action causing milk to sour (see Figure 4.4) in the presence of bacteria which grow at room temperatures (mesophilic bacteria) and is the carbohydrate source for beneficial starter cultures used in yogurts and cheesemaking during which process lactose is converted to lactic acid.

Much of the lactose in cheesemaking remains unaltered and being soluble is drained from the cheese into the whey. In recent years the whey proteins have been recovered by ultrafiltration and the lactose has been collected and hydrolysed to produce glucose/galactose for use as a sweetening agent in confectionery. Lactose itself is used in the pharmaceutical industry for coating pills.

There are wide ranges of methods used to measure lactose. The chloramine-T test is a typical redox method in which, after removal of fat and protein by precipitation with tungstic acid (an allowance is made to the volume effect of different fat and protein values), lactose is oxidised using hypo-iodite produced from the action of potassium iodide and chloramine-T. After acidification any hypo-iodite remaining after the oxidation of lactose is titrated as iodine using a standard solution of sodium thiosulphate with starch as an indicator.

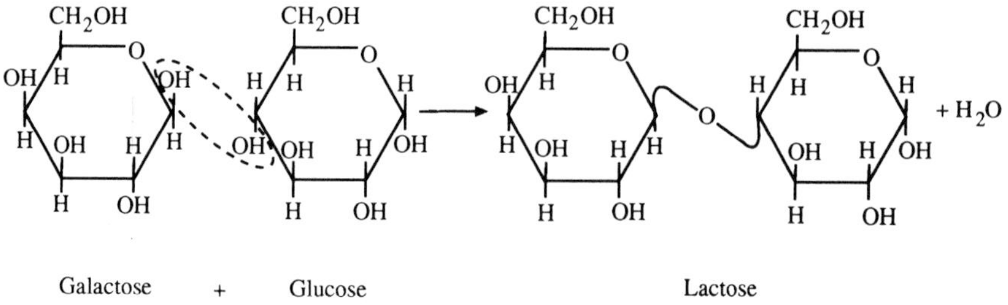

Figure 6.6 Structure of lactose molecule.

Polarimetry is also used and involves measurement of the optical rotation of the filtrate of milk from which fat and protein have been removed by precipitation with a zinc acetate mixture followed by filtration. The observed optical rotation at a wavelength of 589.44 nm is compared with that of a standard lactose solution to give a measure of the lactose in the sample.

Enzymic methods have become more widely used in recent years since they are specific. The two previous methods can be affected by the presence of oxidising or reducing agents or optically active materials other than lactose. In the enzymic method, which is specific to lactose, the disaccharide is hydrolysed by β-galactosidase to produce glucose and β-galactose and either of these can be quantified to give a measure of the original lactose in the sample.

High performance liquid chromatography (HPLC) may also be used to determine lactose in milk. The sugar is separated using an analytical column (a cation exchange column is particularly effective) and when released it is measured by a refractive index detector.

The most widely used routine method of measuring lactose in milk is by means of infrared absorption where fat, protein and lactose are all measured. However, being a secondary method it is dependent on the accuracy of calibration against one of the above reference methods.

6.5   The use of instruments in assessing compositional quality

Reference testing of milk for compositional quality is rather lengthy, labour-intensive and expensive making such methods unsuitable for routine use in quality control, in quality payment or in dairy herd improvement laboratories where large numbers of samples have to be tested. The needs of these areas for low cost, high throughput test methods to provide quick test results in a form which allows data to be handled automatically led to the development of instrumental methods of analysis in the 1960s. It is interesting to trace the development of these instruments which has led to the dairy industry now being provided with a wide family of instruments of varying cost and versatility capable of meeting the industry's many specific needs, from manual sample presentation for small laboratories through to fully automated instruments with automatic data capture for mass testing laboratories and even to fully on-line instruments for process control.

The early instruments were based on mechanised stoichiometric reactions requiring specific volumes of reagents to be mixed with a specific volume of milk. The best and earliest example of these is the Milko-tester (Foss Electric, Denmark). The principle of this instrument is that the cloudiness or turbidity, caused when milk is added to water, is due jointly to the fat and to casein micelles—part of the protein. By solubilising the casein micelle with EDTA the turbidity becomes dependent only on the fat, but is affected by both the number and size of the fat globules. Fat globules are reduced to a common size by homogenisation thus giving a turbidity related directly to the fat percentage. In the early 1960s Foss Electric produced their Mark II Milko-tester. This required about 75 ml of milk to be homogenised. A portion was then mixed with a diluent to solubilise the casein, and the fat was directly determined by measuring its turbidity. This Mark II Milko-tester could be used only for determining fat in milk. This was a disadvantage and tended to restrict the potential sale of the instrument.

Foss therefore introduced the Mark III Milko-tester. This benefited from a number of developments and improvements which made it capable of being used for measuring fat in milk, cream, skim-milk, yogurt, cheese, and many other products.

The Milko-tester was the basis of the mass laboratory testing when Foss produced the Milko-tester automatic. This had automatic sample feed and measured fat in milk at a rate of about 240 samples/h. This was particularly valuable in areas such as dairy herd improvement or quality payment where large numbers of samples have to be tested with a very low labour input. The high capital cost of the automatic instrument was counterbalanced by its high sample throughput, low labour demand, and low chemical costs, making the overall cost per test lower than that for either conventional chemical methods or manual instruments.

The Milko-tester principle was also used in the process control area when equipment was developed to automatically standardise fat in liquid milk. Once every 20 s the instrument automatically samples blended milk from a line leading from two storage vats, one containing whole milk and the other skim-milk. The Milko-tester was set at, say, a 3.5% fat requirement, so that if the fat in the blend of skim-milk and whole milk fell below 3.5% a signal from the Milko-tester automatically closed down the valve in the skim-milk line, hence reducing the ratio of skimmed to whole milk and increasing the fat percentage of the mixture. If the fat percentage rose above 3.5% a signal from the Milko-tester opened the valve in the skim-milk line, hence reducing the fat percentage of the mixture. This simple use of the output from the Milko-tester continuously blended skim-milk and whole milk to give a 3.5% fat mixture irrespective of the fat percentage of the raw milk held in the milk silo.

The simple Milko-tester principle of turbidimetric measurement has therefore been engineered to satisfy demands in the creamery laboratory, the mass testing laboratory and for on-line process control.

Interest in protein testing saw the development of a parallel group of instruments based on dye-binding techniques. Sulphonated dyes react quantitatively with proteins at low pH to form insoluble protein–dye complexes.

The principle of the method is that a standardised solution of Amido Black dye, buffered to pH 2.4, is added to an aliquot of milk. The insoluble dye–protein complex formed is removed by filtration or centrifugation and the intensity of colour of the remaining solution assessed by measuring its absorbance at wavelength in the range 550–620 nm. The absorbance is inversely related to the protein content of the original milk.

Like the Milko-tester this principle created a family of instruments. A semiautomatic instrument was used for measuring the protein content of milk in dairy laboratories. For mass testing laboratories a 'combi' unit was produced which synchronised the Milko-tester automatic and the Pro-milk automatic to provide a continuous fat and protein mass testing system which in its day revolutionised mass testing laboratories and offered a means of paying farmers on protein as well as fat. This type of instrumental development represented a quantum leap forward for those laboratories handling large numbers of samples for dairy herd improvement testing.

The mechanisation of stoichiometric methods such as turbidity and dye binding were soon to be replaced by a new generation of equipment based on measurement using infrared absorption which provided cleaner working conditions with no effluent disposal problems since no reagents were involved. In addition, these instruments provided measurements of fat, protein and lactose from a single sample.

6.5.1 Assessing compositional quality using infrared

The principle of using infrared absorption to measure the quality of milk was first proposed by Goulden working at the National Institute for Research in Dairying (Reading, Berkshire, UK).

In examining the absorption of infrared radiation by milk, Goulden noted that its spectrum was different from that of water, which itself gave a very strong absorption. This led Goulden to construct a double beam instrument called the IRMA (infrared milk analyser) which by comparing the absorption of milk with that of water provided a means of measuring the fat, protein and lactose content of the milk. IRMA was commercially developed by Grubb Parsons of Newcastle upon Tyne (UK); since that time considerable improvements have been made in infrared measurement of milk composition.

Modern instruments are single beam, in which the absorption of specific wavelengths of infrared light is used to measure the concentration of fat, protein and lactose in milk. In practice, the absorption is also measured at 'reference' wavelengths. The two values are subtracted from each other to remove the influence of water absorption.

In order to ensure that only the light of the desired wavelength is detected, optical filters (interference filters) which permit only the desired wavelength to pass, are used. The filters are arranged in a filter wheel which rotates to bring each of the filters in turn—two per component—into position in the path of the infrared beam.

Although the wavelengths are carefully chosen, each component also absorbs a small amount of infrared energy at the wavelengths of the others, e.g. although the fat filters mainly detect the presence of fat, small amounts of protein and lactose are also registered by them. Therefore the signals received from each pair of filters will not give a completely accurate value for the concentration of the component concerned. This problem is solved mathematically in a microprocessor by adding to the fat filters' signals a certain percentage of the readings obtained by the protein and lactose filter pairs. The other combinations are similarly compensated for. These corrections are called 'intercorrection factors' and are preset by the manufacturers.

6.5.1.1 Fat.   For fat content the principle of this now widely used infrared analysis of milk involves counting of ester linkages by measuring their infrared absorption (Figure 6.7). The fat molecule consists of a glycerol 'backbone' to which up to three fatty acid chains are bound.

Two different wavelengths, 5.7 μm and 3.5 μm, can be used to determine the fat in milk. The 5.7 μm filter is referred to as Fat A and the 3.5 μm as Fat B.

(1)   *Fat A*
      The absorption at 5.7 μm is due to stretching vibrations in the C=O bonds of the carboxyl group in fat (Figure 6.7). Since there is only one carboxyl group per fatty acid, this measurement 'counts' the number of fat molecules regardless of the carbon chain length

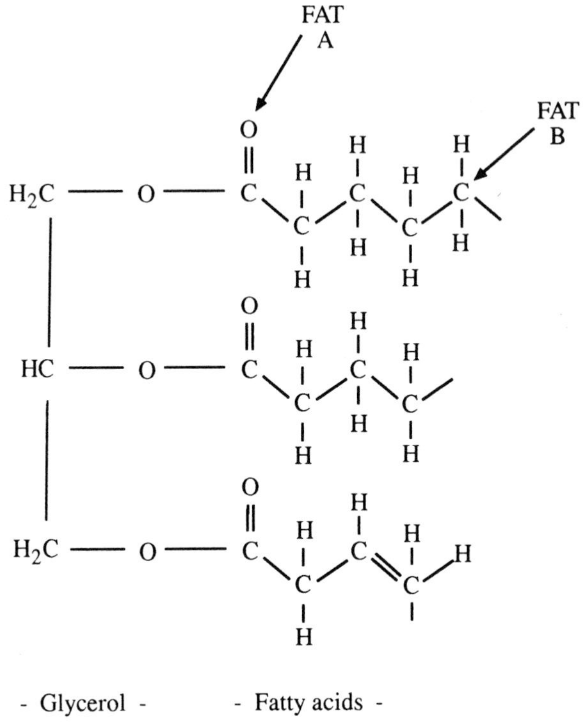

Figure 6.7 Infrared measurement of fat. A, measuring carbonyl; B, measuring ester linkages.

and molecular weight of individual fatty acids.

If the average chain length (mean molecular weight) of the fatty acids is changed, the number of triglyceride molecules per unit weight will change too, and an error will occur in the results unless the change is compensated for by recalibrating the instrument. The composition of butterfat varies with season, region, breed, cow and stage of lactation and this means that an instrument using the 5.7 μm filter must be recalibrated when, for instance, cows go from winter to summer feeds.

Comparisons of infrared against reference gravimetric methods have identified errors associated with band A filters and this resulted in the production of B filters in 1981. B type filters use the CH_2 and CH_3 absorption centres of the fatty acids, which represent 73% of the fat by weight, and are less sensitive to variations in fatty acid chain length and degree of unsaturation.

(2)   *Fat B*

The absorption at 3.5 μm is due to stretching vibrations in the

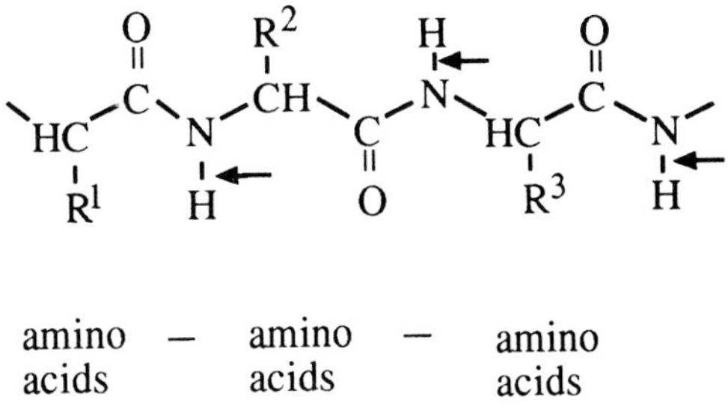

amino — amino — amino
acids   acids   acids

Figure 6.8 Infrared measurement of protein.

saturated C–H bonds of the fatty acid chains (Figure 6.7). This measurement is, therefore, related to both the size and the number of fat molecules in the sample, as the number of carbon–hydrogen bonds increase substantially in proportion to the molecular size.

Measurement at 3.5 μm also includes free fatty acids that may have formed during storage; these are not measured at 5.7 μm.

Protein and lactose contribute to the absorption at 3.5 μm, but their interference is removed by means of suitable intercorrection factors set by the manufacturers of the instrument using an equation that calculates the fat content from the instrument signals.

6.5.1.2. Protein. The protein molecule consists primarily of amino acid units joined together in a long chain by peptide bonds (Figure 6.8).

The wavelength for protein determination is 6.5 μm, and it is the nitrogen-hydrogen bonds within the peptide bonds that are responsible for the infrared absorption. Thus, the measurement represents the number of amino acids rather than their weight, but as the composition of protein in milk is fairly constant, this causes no problems. In contrast to the reference (Kjeldahl) method the infrared measurement does not measure all non-protein nitrogen. It excludes urea and in fact is a measure only of proteinaceous nitrogen.

6.5.1.3 Lactose. Lactose consists of a glucose molecule and a galactose molecule joined together (Figure 6.9). The hydroxyl group (OH) is characteristic of carbohydrates and it is the bond between the hydroxyl group and the carbon atom which absorbs infrared energy at the lactose wavelength, 9.5 μm.

The Milkoscan's 'lactose' determination is not actually specific for lactose, but will measure other carbohydrates containing the OH group which may be present in the sample.

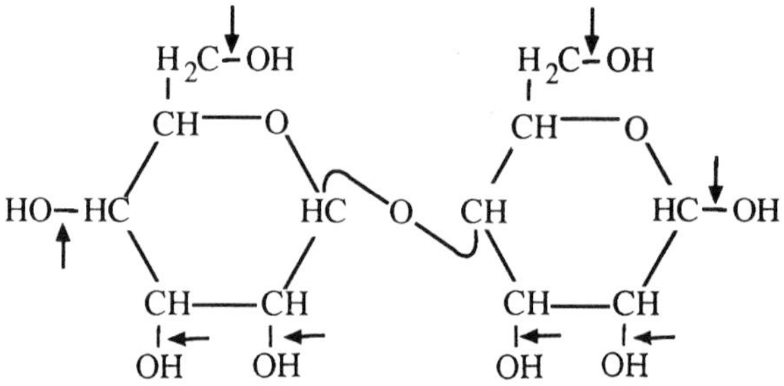

Figure 6.9   Infrared measurement of lactose.

None of these instrumental methods are independent measuring techniques and all have to be calibrated against reference methods. Calibration is achieved by ensuring that instrumental methods give the same results as reference methods, e.g. Rose–Gottlieb for fat, Kjeldahl for protein and polarimetery for lactose over a wide range of quality. Regular calibration checks are therefore needed to maintain instrument accuracy.

Instruments need to be corrected with respect to slope or bias to give the same results as reference techniques. Once calibrated to ensure that the instrument slope is correct bulk reference samples are tested to minimise drifts in the instrumental bias.

These instruments, providing good calibration and calibrated methods are practised, produce accurate, highly reproducible results relatively inexpensively (assuming that the high capital cost can be spread over a large number of samples) and within seconds. The data generated can be captured automatically together with the sample identification which can be read at the point of test from a bar code label attached to the sample bottle. Thus, sample identity, fat, protein and lactose can be read and recorded at a rate of over 300 samples/h. The data can be fed directly to a computer where results may be compared with previous data for that farmer and, if acceptable, stored and used for payment purposes. Where results show an abrupt change in quality the computer can be programmed to send a message to the laboratory, before the sample has been discarded, requesting further tests on that supply (e.g. extraneous water).

On-line infrared instruments are also available for standardising fat and protein in milk fully automatically by blending supplies of high fat/protein and low fat/protein milks to reach a pre-set value as described earlier for the on-line Milko-testers.

6.5.1.4   The future.   Fourier transform infrared (FTIR) is a technique which could lead to a means of measuring fat, protein and lactose in milk without the need for local calibration. The technique lends itself to measurement and quantification not only of fat, protein and lactose but also other chemicals in milk such as citrate which give rise to interfering absorption with existing infrared instruments. If the successful development of FTIR came about, then infrared instruments throughout the world could, in theory, be calibrated with the same basic milk samples. This would make for improved agreement in test results between different countries of the world.

6.6 Dairy herd improvement (DHI) and quality payment laboratories

It is good management practice for farmers to have a measure of the yield and quality (fat and protein) of individual cows within the herd in order to provide them with information to better feed individual cows on performance and to judge the value of the cow for breeding and sale. Such a service is often provided by an independent DHI Authority and these often operate mass testing laboratories, using automatic instrumental methods of analysis.

The yield of an individual cow's milk at the farm is measured by dial scales, vertical sided calibration jars or milk flowmeters. A composite 24 h sample is usually taken, in proportion to the volume produced at evening and morning milking, after air agitation of the milk in the recorder jar. Cost restraints usually demand that samples are chemically preserved before being transported at ambient temperature to the test laboratory.

Lactose determinations made on individual cow samples give a rough indication of mastitis although somatic cell counts are more widely used as they provide a more reliable indication of udder health.

Samples of bulked herd milk are also taken regularly for quality payment purposes. Since test methods and sample transport routes for DHI and quality payment tend to be the same it is usual for the sake of economy for samples to be tested in the same laboratory. Transport of unpreserved quality payment samples usually involves the use of cold boxes. Since the accuracy of test results has a higher commercial impact, sample condition for quality payment is more important than for dairy herd improvement. Samples are often tested not only for compositional quality but also for hygiene and inhibitory substances where preservatives would interfere.

6.7 Quality payment systems for milk

6.7.1 Compositional quality

The two basic objectives of farmer payment schemes are

(1)   to pay farmers differentially according to their milk quality; and

(2)   to use financial penalties or incentives as a means of improving milk quality.

Since the yield of products made from milk is directly related to its compositional quality it is logical to pay farmers more money for high milk solids and less money for low milk solids. The choice of which milk constitutents to pay on and their relative value varies from country to country.

Many payment schemes started by paying on fat only—largely because this was the only parameter for which large numbers of samples could be easily tested. However, as test methods have improved, schemes have become more sophisticated in their attempt to encourage farmers to provide the right milk quality for different market needs.

In the UK payment schemes have moved from 'Fat only' through 'Fat and SNF' to 'Fat, protein and lactose' where the relative payments for 'Fat, protein and lactose' are regularly changed to reflect their market value. Thus, in the UK the value of fat to farmers has decreased and that of protein has increased in line with changes in market values and changes in consumption patterns. Some Scandinavian countries have ceased to pay anything on fat and now pay only on protein. France pay on fat and protein where protein is recorded as 'true', not total protein, and it is likely that if direct measurement of casein were available those involved in cheesemaking would pay on fat and casein. The way in which farmers' payments on compositional quality are built up therefore depends on the anticipated end-use for that milk. Compositional payment schemes therefore target to pay farmers on the weight of milk solids derived from measurement of volume and percentage 'milk solids'.

Payment on kg of 'milk solids' may not in itself be entirely fair. The same weight of milk solids 'diluted' by more water, it could be argued, is worth less than that weight of milk solids in a more concentrated form. After all it costs more in transportation, storage and evaporation costs to treat the more dilute solids. It is for this reason that some countries also introduce a 'negative payment' for volume which attempts to compensate the farmer producing higher milk solids per litre in consideration of the cost benefits that his more concentrated supply brings to the haulier and processor.

The second objective of payment schemes is to encourage producers to improve milk quality. This is usually achieved by applying bonuses and/or penalties based on quality tests.

This is a 'carrot and stick' approach used to dissuade farmers from producing milk of 'undesirable quality' such as high bacterial count, the presence of dirt, undesirable flavour, etc.

The parameter chosen and the penalty applied depend on the particular market requirement.

The most common penalty schemes are targeted to achieve improvements in hygienic quality, control of antibiotic residues and somatic cells.

6.7.1.1 Hygienic quality. A good hygienic level of milk production at the farm is essential.

Here, the test method will generally be an indicator of microbiological contamination. Since milk leaving the healthy udder is virtually free from bacteria, the total bacterial count or an equivalent measurement is often taken as an indication of good hygienic milking practice.

The level of total bacterial count (TBC) at which a penalty is levied on milk varies considerably from country to country and can be set according to the hygienic production conditions prevailing with progressive tightening of the standard as quality is improved. Many countries set penalties at 200 000 organisms/ml or even 100 000 organisms/ml.

It is, however, desirable to keep bacterial counts low and it is known that with good hygienic practice, an average TBC of 10 000 organisms/ml can be achieved. It is for this reason that some countries not only penalise poor quality milk but also offer a premium for milk of high hygienic quality.

6.7.1.2 Control of antibiotic residues. It is generally accepted that milk should be free from antibiotic residues, since these may give rise to product faults by inhibiting the growth of microorganisms used to produce cultured products such as yogurt or cheese, or may cause human health problems such as allergy or the development of antibiotic resistant pathogens. Regular testing for antibiotics is therefore practised, with severe penalties being applied when positive results are obtained.

A conflict of standards can sometimes exist in that the legal upper limit set by law is that set for toxicological reasons. However, lower concentrations than these may inhibit cheese or yogurt cultures and for this reason a particular processor may be forced to adopt more strict standards.

6.7.1.3 Somatic cells. Somatic cell counts (SCC) are an indication of udder health. The presence of somatic cells in milk is also undesirable and may give rise to product problems, hence many countries include penalties for high SCC in payment schemes.

References amd further reading

APHA (1985) *Standard Methods for the Examination of Dairy Products* (15th edn.). American Public Health Association, Washington, DC, USA.

Campbell and Marshall (1975) *The Science of Providing Milk for Man*. McGraw-Hill, New York, USA.

Davis, J.G. (1959) The laboratory control of milk. *Milk Testing* (2nd edn). Dairy Industries Ltd, 9 Crough Square, Fleet Street, London EC4.

Emmons, D. B., Tulloch, D. and Ernstrom, C. A. (1990a) Product-yield pricing system. 1. Technological considerations in multi-component pricing of milk. *J. Dairy Sci.*, **73**, 1712.

Emmons, D.B., Tulloch, D. and Ernstrom, C.A. (1990b) Product-yield pricing system. 2. Plant considerations in multi-product pricing of milk. *J. Dairy Sci.,* **73**, 1724.

Goulden, J.D. (1964) *Soc. J. Dairy Res.*, **31**, 273.

Grappin, R. and Jeunet, R. (1972) Facteurs biologiques responsables des variations observées dans la précision des méthodes de routine utilisées pour le dosage de la matière grasse du lait. *Le Lait*, **52** (5–6), 324.

Hall, A.J. (1970) Seasonal and regional variations in the fatty acid composition of milk fat. *Dairy Ind.*, **35**, 1.

Harding, F. (1989) The impact of central testing on milk quality. *Dairy Ind. Int.*, **52** (1) 17.

Harding, F. and Royal, J.H.L. (1974a). Variations in the composition of bulked milk in England and Wales during the period 1947 to 1970. *Dairy Ind.*, **39**(8), 294.

Harding, F. and Royal, J.H.L. (1974b) Variations in the nitrogen-containing fractions of bulked milk in England and Wales during the period 1947 to 1970. *Dairy Ind.*, October, 342–378.

Kroger, M. (1971) Instrumental milk fat determination. Effects of potassium dichromate concentration and sample storage time on milko-tester results. *J. Dairy Sci.*, **54**, 735.

McGann, T.C.A. (1970) *Dairy Ind.*, **35**(10), 671.

Rowland, S.J. (1938) The precipitation of the protein of milk. *J. Dairy Res.*, **9**, 30.

Walstra, P. and Jennes, R. (1984) *Dairy Chemistry and Physics*. John Wiley & Sons, New York, USA.

7 Milk from sheep and goats

F. HARDING

7.1 Introduction

Most of the data in this book, whilst written for cow's (bovine) milk, equally applies to sheep's (ovine) and to goat's (caprine) milk.

Of the total world production of milk (Table 7.1), cows produce about 90.8%, sheep 1.7%, goats 1.5% and buffalo 6%. Milk from other species, such as camels, is also creating interest. However, this chapter will be limited to comparing the quality issues of sheep's, goat's and cow's milks, since these three species provide the most significant source of milk for commercial production.

Sheep and goats have been used as a source of milk for thousands of years and whilst usually limited to areas where climatic conditions prevent cattle from being kept, there is a growing interest in sheep's and goat's milk products more generally. This widening interest is to some extent due to successful marketing of specialist goat and sheep cheeses and to some extent due to the restrictions created by quotas placed on cow's milk but not on other species.

7.2 Milking practices

The milk ejection reflex of sheep and goats is very similar to that described for cows. First of all the udder stimulation causes a nervous reflex; the hormone oxytocin is produced, which is transported to the udder, and milk flows.

Mechanical milking of sheep and goats came much later than cows. Historically, most sheep and goat herds were small and free grazing was common. Hence, hand milking was, and still is in many countries, widely practised. The first milking machine for sheep was made in 1932 with the objective of improving the bacteriological quality. Mechanical milking grew in the 1950s and 1960s as the benefits became obvious. The design was based on those developed for cows with modifications to meet the special characteristics for sheep and goat; goats, for example, have two rather than four teats.

Mechanical milking brings a number of benefits. Animals are milked in a parlour with a clean concrete floor rather than in a field. This benefits

Table 7.1   World production of milk[a]

	Million tons
Cow's milk	427.9
Buffalo's milk	27.2
Sheep's milk	7.6
Goat's milk	7.2

[a]Source: FAO (1981).

Table 7.2   Typical composition of cow's, sheep's and goat's milk

	Fat (%)	Protein (%)	Lactose (%)	Ash (%)	Total solids (%)
Cows	3.9	3.2	4.6	0.72	12.6
Sheep	7.1	5.7	4.6	0.93	18.2
Goats	3.6	3.3	4.6	0.80	12.1

milk hygiene and enables the milker to monitor animal health and individual animal milk yield. As with cows, animal health is important as is good hygienic milking practice. Since most sheep's and goat's milk products are made from raw milk it could be argued that animal health is even more important than with cows. Mastitis is not an uncommon udder disease and those precautions advised to limit the spread of the disease in cows also apply to sheep and goats.

7.3   Compositional quality

One of the most significant differences between milk from sheep and the other two species is its compositional quality. As with cow's milk the composition for the other species will vary with different breeds within a species, within a lactation, with feeding practices and with animal health. The effect of diet on goat's milk production is very similar to that of the cow. A comparison of compositional quality can be made based on average figures as seen in Table 7.2.

The gross composition of goat's milk is close to that of cow's. However, milk from sheep has a much higher fat and protein content. This is advantageous to the processor in terms of yield since most sheep's milk is made into cheese. Traditional cheeses such as Roquefort, Feta and Manchego, made from sheep's and goat's milk, are known throughout the world and have contributed to a higher value being attributed to sheep and goat's milk than to cow's milk. There is therefore a need to have analytical methods capable of detecting the addition of cow's milk to that of the other species.

Sheep's milk fat is always white whereas cow's milk fat, especially where cows are pasture fed, is a yellow creamy colour, since it contains a large proportion of carotenoids. Feta cheese, made from sheep's milk, is traditionally white thus making it difficult to make Feta from cow's milk without having to 'bleach' the fat.

7.4 Measuring cow's milk in sheep's or goat's milk products

7.4.1 Differences in lipids

Fat from sheep's, goat's and cow's milk contains a high proportion of low-molecular-weight fatty acids with an even number of carbon atoms. Sheep's and goat's milk however contain a larger proportion of $C_{6:0}$ (caproic); $C_{8:0}$ (caprylic); $C_{10:0}$ (capric) and $C_{12:0}$ (lauric) acids. Much work has been undertaken on devising correlations of fatty acids against published data as a basis for detecting the presence of cow's milk in sheep or goat's milk products. Chromatography is used to quantify the free fatty acids in the product. The level of detection of cow's milk reported varies considerably, with a range of 5–15%, due to natural variations in fatty acid composition.

7.4.2 Differences in protein

Electrophoresis has been used to separate caseins and on polyacrylamide gel and starch gel; the α_{S1}-casein from cow's milk is more mobile than that from goat's milk. It is suggested that a 1% mixture of cow's milk could be detected. The breakdown of casein in matured cheeses, however, tends to limit the use of such methods, based on protein separation, to milk rather than cheeses.

7.4.3 Immunological techniques

These methods are based on antigen–antibody precipitation reactions which differ for different proteins from different species. Now that difficulties associated with preparing anti-cow's milk serum have been resolved, it is possible to measure low levels of cow's milk in goat's, sheep's or buffalo's milk by this technique.

7.4.4 General differences

Alkaline phosphatase (ALP) is used with cow's milk as the end product test to ascertain that effective pasteurisation has taken place. The pool of

Table 7.3 Distribution of nitrogen fractions as a percentage of total nitrogen in cow's, sheep's and goat's milk[a]

	Cow's	Sheep's	Goat's
Casein	77.8	78.5	75.6
Whey protein	17.0	16.8	15.7
NPN	5.2	4.7	8.7

[a]Source: IDF (1986).

ALP in cow's milk is about 3300 µg phenol/ml. The level of ALP in raw sheep's milk is three to four times higher than in cow's milk and that in goat's milk is some four-fold lower. These differences have to be taken into account in the interpretation of the test (chapter 9).

Studies of goat's milk have shown a lower initial pool of ALP with machine milking than with hand milking. The difference is due to microbial phosphatase owing to the higher bacterial count occurring with handling milking. Microbial phosphatase, being more heat stable than natural phosphatase, will remain after pasteurisation and can give rise to a false positive ALP test suggesting that milk has not been correctly heat treated. The ALP limit for goat's milk is 0.67 µg phenol/ml.

Lipase found in goat's milk, unlike that in cow's milk correlates closely to spontaneous lipolysis and can play a major role in flavour impairment even at low storage temperatures.

7.5   Instrumental methods of analysis

Chapter 6 described indirect methods of analysis such as infrared for the measurement of fat, protein and lactose in cow's milk. These methods can also be used for analysis of sheep's and goat's milk. However, instruments need to be calibrated against reference methods using samples of milk from the species under test. The reasons for this are two-fold. Firstly, for protein measurement there are differences in the make up of total nitrogen as determined by Kjeldahl (section 6.4.2—proteins).

The variation in non-protein nitrogen (NPN) will affect the comparison of the reference and indirect methods thus making it important that the calibration of instruments is made on the same population of milks being tested routinely (Table 7.3).

The second reason is the wider range of values for fat and protein observed, especially for sheep's milk, and differences between species which affect the indirect method such as refractive index of fat and differences in infrared absorbtion between the species.

References and further reading

Bret, G. (1968) *Use of Electrophoresis for the Identification of Mixtures of Cow's, Ewe's and Goat's Milks in Dairy Products* (Annual Bulletin, part VII). Brussels, Belgium.

Ely, E. and Peterson, W.E. (1941) Factors involved in the ejection of milk. *J. Dairy Sci.*, **24**, 211–223.

FAO (1981) *Production Year Book (Vol. 34): FAO Statistics series No. 34*. FAO, Rome, Italy.

FAO *Technology of Traditional Milk Products in Developing Countries* (Publication No. 85). FAO, Rome, Italy.

Foissy (1976) Methods for differentiating milk from different animals. *Oesterrichische, Milch-wirtshaft*, **31**, 5–8.

Gombocz, E. *et al.* (1991) Immunological detection of cow's milk casein in ewe's milk cheese. *Z. Lebensm. Unters Forsch.*, **172**, 178–181

IDF (1981) *Buffalo as a Candidate for Milk Production* (Bulletin 137). IDF, Brussels, Belgium.

IDF (1983a) *Production and Utilisation of Goat's and Ewe's Milk* (Bulletin 158). IDF, Brussels, Belgium.

IDF (1983b) *Goat's and Ewe's Milk Cheeses from Seven Countries* (Document 158). IDF, Brussels, Belgium.

IDF (1984) *Update on Existing Analytical Methods for Detecting Mixtures of Cow's, Ewe's and Goat's Milk* (Bulletin 181). IDF, Brussels, Belgium.

IDF (1986) *Production and Utilisation of Ewe's and Goat's Milk* (Bulletin 202). IDF, Brussels, Belgium.

Juarez, M. *et al.* (1978) Estudio sombre la compoicion de la leche de vaca en Espana Instituto de Productos Lacteos. Arganda (Madrid)

Krause, I. *et al.* (1982) Detection of cow's milk in sheep's milk and goat's milk and cheese by isoelectric focussing on thin layers of polyacrylamide gels containing urea. *Z. Lebensm. Unters Forsch.*, **174**, 195–199.

Morland-Fehr and Sauvant (1980) Composition and yield of goat's milk as affected by nutritional manipulation. *J. Dairy Sci.*, **63**, 1671–1680.

Ramos, M. and Juarez, M. (1981) *The Composition of Ewe's and Goat's Milk* (Bulletin 140). IDF, Brussels, Belgium.

8 The impact of raw milk quality on product quality
F. HARDING

8.1 Introduction

The saying 'you can't make a silk purse out of a sow's ear' is true of milk processing. The quality of the starting raw milk has a very definite effect on the yield and quality of products made from it. The compositional quality, the hygienic quality, the health of the cow in terms of mastitis and the level of contaminants present can all have an impact on the yield and/or quality, and hence financial return from products made from milk. This chapter summarises the impact of raw milk quality on the yield and quality of products made from it.

8.2 Compositional quality

The most obvious raw milk quality attribute to affect products is compositional quality. The simplest case is the production of butter. Butter has a legal minimum of 80% butterfat and a legal maximum of 16% water content. Non-salted butter therefore will have an approximate composition of

$$\begin{array}{cccc} & \text{Moisture} & \text{'curd'} & \text{Fat} \\ \text{Butter} = & 16\% \, + & 1.4\% \, + & 82.6\% \quad = 100\% \end{array}$$

(note the moisture derives from 16% skim-milk at 9.00% solids-not-fat (SNF), giving 1.4% SNF as 'curd' in butter)

Clearly a farmer producing milk of 3.0% fat would need to consign more litres of milk than one producing milk of say 3.9% fat to produce the same amount of butter. One can calculate that at 3.0% fat you need 30 355 litres of milk to produce 1 tonne of butter whereas at 3.9% fat you only need 23 350 litres. Clearly a butter maker is not going to pay the same price for a litre of milk at 3.00% fat as he would for 3.90% fat. Similarly, SNF is important in skim-milk powder production—a supply with an SNF of 8.2% will yield roughly 5% less powder than one of a milk of 8.6% SNF.

For cheese, the yield is dependent on levels of fat and casein in milk. However, since fat is entrapped in casein, the fat to casein ratio in the original milk also important to the cheesemaker otherwise too high a fat content gives rise to fat lost to whey. These days milk is usually standardised to a constant fat to casein ratio (approximately 0.7:1 in Cheddar cheese) to achieve an optimal fat recovery and the desired moisture level in the cheese. Since the economic value of casein is about 1.5 times that of fat the more important component to the cheesemaker is a high casein in milk. Casein is also the quality parameter which affects the yield of cottage (fat-free) cheese. The processor may also use processing techniques to increase cheese yield, for example, by incorporating heat denatured whey proteins, or the butter maker may increase the curd (SNF) content of butter to reduce the more costly butterfat element close to the 80% minimum whilst not exceeding the 16% maximum moisture level, but such effects on product yield are outside the remit of this book.

More dilute milk solids are more expensive to transport, store and concentrate and the yield of products are affected by the percentage of component in the starting material—the raw milk. The yield of specific products being manufactured is of utmost economic importance to the processor. For these reasons farmers are paid on compositional quality and it is important that extraneous water, which dilutes milk constituents, is strictly controlled.

8.3   Opportunities for manipulation of compositional quality

8.3.1   Fat

The type of milk fat produced by cows can be influenced by dietary changes. Milk fats containing a higher proportion of unsaturated fats have been produced by feeding cows with unsaturated fats encapsulated with protein which protects the fat from being saturated in the cows' rumen. Questions need to be asked by the farmer as to the economics of such feeding systems and by the processor as to the susceptibility of these fats to oxidative rancidity. Softer fats, higher in monounsaturated fats, have also been produced by feeding high oil oats to dairy cows. The desire for a greater proportion of unsaturated fats was inspired partially by human dietary concerns about saturated fat consumption, which have now somewhat moderated, and partially by the desire to produce a more spreadable butter. More spreadable butters have also been produced by fractionation of butterfat by the processor.

8.3.2   Protein

It is much more difficult to manipulate the protein content of milk than the fat content. Excess feed only results in a modest increase in protein levels. The potential for increasing the protein content at the expense of fat is therefore limited.

There is however increasing interest in the genetic selection of cows with the κ-casein BB variant since it is believed that such milk has yield advantages in cheesemaking. Considerable work has been undertaken on this topic at the Hannah Research Institute (Ayr, UK) where it has been shown that whilst milk of this genotype does give yield and product quality benefits, the economics of this genetic selection are as yet far from clear.

8.4   The effect of raw milk hygienic quality on product quality

Maintaining high standards of raw milk quality is important, not only because it gives greater flexibility to the processor in terms of holding milk prior to processing but most importantly because of the impact it ultimately has on product quality.

Milk produced under careless conditions can contain a wide range of bacteria; pathogens (*Salmonella, Listeria*, etc.) from faecal contamination; pathogens from udder infection (streptococcal organisms) and milk-spoilage organisms which may be mesophilic, psychrotrophic or thermoduric. The type of organisms which will develop and predominate will depend on the storage time–temperature history of the milk.

Where milk is stored at ambient temperature and collected in cans, mesophilic bacteria tend to predominate. These produce lactic acid from lactose. The production of lactic acid can give rise to problems where milk has to be heated. High acidity can cause curdling of casein when milk is heated. Milk powders, especially those used for recombination, tend to have specifications with upper limits for developed acidity, hence high acidity of raw milk can lead to downgrading of powders with resultant price penalties.

Whilst bulk collection, involving cooling of milk on farms, has eliminated problems associated with acid formers, other organisms, psychrotrops, can, albeit more slowly, grow and cause problems with products made from the milk.

A number of surveys have been undertaken to study the incidence of psychrotrophic sporeformers in farm milk with results showing a range between 25 and 90%. Certainly the incidence in spring and summer is highest with 30–40% of creamery silos containing psychrotrophic *Bacillus* spp.

The major *Bacillus* spp. found is *B. cereus* with *B. circulans* and *B. mycoides* being the other major species. The heat resistance of different species does not vary greatly, whether the spores are present in skimmilk, semi-skimmed, or whole milk or cream, although spores of *B.*

brevis have been shown to be more resistant to heating when they were suspended in double cream where the high lipid content exerts a protective effect.

Studies of this outgrowth of spores in pasteurised products showed growth patterns to be similar in skim-milk, whole milk, single and double cream. Whilst optimum germination and growth temperatures are relatively high (15°C) growth is possible at as low as 6°C with generation times of 7–23 h. There is virtually no growth at 2°C and below except for *B. circulans*.

The growth of psychrotrophic spore formers in pasteurised products can be inhibited by addition of Nisin, a polypeptide antimicrobial. This is, however, only effective where Gram-negative psychrotrophs, i.e. post-pasteurisation contamination, organisms are absent, furthermore its use would offend the 'natural' image of pasteurised milk. Lysozyme, which occurs naturally in milk and has been used for controlling *Clostridum* spp. in milk for cheesemaking, has been shown to be ineffective against most *Bacillus* spp. Heat treatment of 95°C for 15 s has been used to activate *Bacillus* spores and if followed, some 24 h later after storage at 8°C, by a second heat treatment of 80°C for 10 min, results in a significant reduction in spore counts. Removal of spores by bactofugation or a microfiltration technique have been used commercially.

However, such treatments have not found commercial application on a wide scale and since prevention is better than cure, attempts have been made to identify and reduce incidence of spores in raw milk. It has been suggested that inadequate cleaning of the bulk tank is the main source of psychrotrophic *Bacillus* spores although some work in the UK has also implicated contamination of cows teats during grazing.

Whilst there is no connection between the total bacterial count of milk and the spore count for individual farms, it was found in the UK that when the total bacterial count of the national milk supply was improved, through quality payment schemes, the thermoduric count also improved in similar proportions due, it is believed, to the fact that farmers generally took more care in overall milk production hygiene in the attempt to gain bonus for high quality (less than 20 000 organisms/ml) milk.

8.5 Animal health

Animals in bad health are liable to contaminate milk with pathogens, either from direct introduction of pathogens in the udder or by heavy faecal contamination of the milking environment causing secondary contamination of milk. Either way a milking animal's poor health is a threat to the milk supply and ultimately a threat to the consumer. Contamination by *Escherichia coli* is often taken as an indication of faecal contamination, which can give rise to the introduction of *Salmonella, Listeria* and *Campylobacter*—all food-poisoning organisms.

Mycobacterium tuberculosis, the organism causing tuberculosis (TB) in man may also be present in milk unless the herd is TB accredited and *Brucella abortus* can give rise to undulant fever if consumed in milk.

There is therefore a risk with raw milk and products produced from raw milk of the presence of pathogens. They can survive and, if conditions are favourable, even grow causing a public health threat.

Listeria monocytogenes will multiply rapidly in soft, mould ripened cheese where the high pH of the cheese favours the organisms. Fortunately, most of these pathogens are killed by normal pasteurisation time–temperature conditions. Generally, therefore, heat treatment of milk to a minimum time–temperature combination equal to pasteurisation is desirable to minimise risk. If raw milk or products made from it are to be consumed, great care is needed in terms of controlling animal health in order to reduce the risk of presence of pathogens as much as possible. However, some organisms will survive pasteurisation (*Bacillus* spp.) and may, under optimum conditions, produce toxins harmful to man.

8.5.1 *Mastitis*

Not only is mastitis milk a risk with respect to the pathogenic organisms it contains, but mastitic milk may already be chemically changed or contain enzymes capable of creating further damage at a later stage. It has been shown that lipolytic damage to milk fat and proteolytic damage to milk casein occurs in the udder prior to milking, during mastitis infection. Furthermore, mastitic milk has a higher susceptibility to further damage at a later stage.

Lipolysis of milk fat produces free fatty acids which act as foam depressants which depress the whipping properties of cream and the performance of milk in cappuccino coffee. Mastitic milk is characterised by a high somatic cell count (SCC); a significant correlation has been reported between SCC and low flavour scores on pasteurised products.

Diacetyl production, a favourable characteristic in milk products, has been shown to be inhibited hence impairing flavour in fermented products such as yogurt when high (over 500 000 cells/ml) SCC milk is used. Camembert and Tilsit cheeses made from milk with a high SCC (over 600 000 cells/ml) have a bitter flavour which becomes more pronounced during ripening.

It is clear that mastitis is a disease which is costly to the producer in terms of loss of milk yield and quality and to the processor since in general high SCC count milk produces lower quality products in terms of flavour, shelf-life and yield.

The impact of mastitic milk on cheese yield is well recorded. Milk casein is depleted and high fat and protein losses occur in cheesemaking with generally a higher moisture cheese resulting. The level of somatic cells at which major problems occur is not well defined but some workers have concluded that milk with a SCC above 100 000 will have a negative impact on cheese yield and quality.

8.6   Physical handling of milk

Severe pumping and turbulent flow should be avoided since they can cause churning of the fat. The fat globule membrane is susceptible to damage and liberation of the naturally occurring lipoprotein lipase giving rise to flavour impairment. Excessive pumping or agitation of milk should therefore be avoided, and design of pipelines for milk movement is critical. The damage can be exacerbated by changes in chemical conditions such as freezing–thawing or when warm milk from a second milking is added to cold milk from the first milking.

8.7   Taints and contaminants

Milk may contain feeding taints (turnips, kale, garlic, etc.) which may be transient but may also be transferred to milk products. Chemical taints such as chlorophenol taints are a greater potential source of problem in milk products as such taints are permanent and may give unacceptable chemical flavours (chapter 5).

8.8   Pasteurised milk and cream

Clearly the shelf-life of pasteurised milk depends on the numbers and types of microorganisms present and upon the storage temperatures. Work in the UK in the mid-1980s showed that the major factor limiting the shelf-life of pasteurised milk was bacteria introduced through post-pasteurisation contamination. The presence of psychrotrophic Gram-negative rods (GNR) coupled with poor temperature control will severely reduce shelf-life of pasteurised milk. Even very low levels of post-heat treatment contamination (less than 1 GNR/100 ml) can multiply rapidly unless storage temperatures are strictly controlled.

Where post-pasteurisation contamination is controlled however organisms capable of surviving heat treatment and subsequently growing even at refrigerated temperatures, become the limiting factor in shelf-life. These organisms are mainly Gram-positive sporeforming bacteria of the genus

Bacillus. Work at the Hannah Research Institute (Ayr, UK) has shown that the number of *Bacillus* spores in milk varies seasonally being highest in the summer–early autumn (July–October) at which time there is also an increase in concentration of a naturally occurring germinant in milk.

It should be remembered that bacteria will be significantly higher in cream than in skim-milk, since bacteria tend to be entangled in fat and hence be concentrated during the separation stage.

The level of psychrotrops in milk should be kept as low as possible to avoid product faults. Care should especially be taken to keep storage temperatures low during times of highest risk (summer and early autumn).

8.8.1   Summary of action to limit problems in pasteurised products

(1) Eliminate post-pasteurisation contamination.
(2) Maintain strict low temperature control of pasteurised products since organisms which survive pasteurisation will grow, albeit slowly, at low temperatures.
(3) Maintain good temperature control and hygienic quality control of plant and milk at production, transport and storage prior to processing.
(4) Offer farmers financial incentives for producing top quality, i.e. better than (20 000 organisms/ml) milk. This should also reduce the level of thermoduric bacteria in milk.
(5) Avoid storing milk for long periods of time prior to processing.

8.9   UHT products

Some psychrotrophs (*Pseudomonas*) can produce extracellular heat-stable enzymes capable of breaking down proteins and fats. The heat stability of some of these enzymes is so great that they can survive pasteurisation, UHT treatment and in some cases even sterilisation. Extending the storage times of milk either on the farm or at the processing centre therefore has inherent risks. Lengthening storage times should only be considered where deep cooling or other means of limiting psychrotrophic growth is practised.

If the psychrotrophic count of raw milk is allowed to reach levels over 10/ml, UHT products obtained from it will have a reduced shelf-life. Shelf-life impairment can be due to development of 'off-flavours' or gelation, the development of which depends to some extent upon the storage temperature of the UHT product. UHT skim-milk stored at 20°C has a shelf-life of at least 4 months but this will be significantly lower in hot climates. Germination of spores of *Bacillus* spp. is optimum at 15°C and whilst many strains are capable of growth at 2°C generation times are long (18–36 h compared with 7–23 h at 6°C storage. Whilst UHT products are ambient temperature products, clearly the presence of spores does make some attempt at reduced temperature control desirable, especially in high fat products when sporulation appears to be greater.

There is a need for the dairy industry to have more rapid and more sensitive means of measuring heat resistant enzymes in milk in order to have a better means of controlling the impact on UHT product quality.

8.10   Cheese

It was recognised over 10 000 years ago that one of the most efficient ways of preserving milk was to convert it into cheese. Storage or transport of milk in the stomachs of animals in warm climates led to the development of rennet cheeses, and preservation of milk by sun drying in warm climates it is believed gave rise to the first acid coagulated cheeses. Cheesemaking is now a major industry with over 900 individual types of cheese utilising about one-third of the world's milk production yielding well over 12.5 million tonnes of cheese a year. Whilst cow's milk is used to produce most of the world's cheese nearly all of the sheep's and goat's milk produced finds its way into cheese production.

8.10.1   Impact of milk quality

The chemical composition and microbiological quality of milk used in cheesemaking will influence both the yield and quality of cheese produced. Raw milk chemical composition will have an effect on renneting, cheese yield and its body and texture. As discussed earlier, casein levels in raw milk are critically important in determining yield. Casein to fat ratios in cheese milk are normally standardised at 0.7:1.

Since casein levels and quality are affected by mastitis, herd health is important for milk destined for cheesemaking. The absence of antibiotics and other antimicrobials is also critically important to the cheesemaker as their presence can severely inhibit the starter cultures used. Microbiological quality of the raw milk is also important. Milk for cheesemaking is often cold stored prior to manufacture. If milk is not stored at low temperatures (below 5°C) psychrotrophic organisms (*Pseudomonas, Enterobacter*, etc.) will grow and produce extracellular enzymes which, even though the bacteria producing them are killed, survive the heat treatment. The proteases produced can give rise to cheese yield losses of 5% or more in soft cheeses with raw milk counts of 10^6. Lipases give rise to rancid flavours in cheese hence storage conditions aimed at limiting bacterial growth are important (chapter 4).

Further reading

Compositional quality

Banks, W. Clapperton, J.L. and Kelly, M.E. (1980) Effect of oil-enriched diets on the milk yield and composition and on the composition and physical properties of the milk fat of cows receiving a basal ration of grass silage. *J. Dairy Res.*, **47**, 277–285.

Callanan, T. and Lewis, K. (1983) Milk compositional quality—Cheddar cheese yields. *Proceedings of IDF Symposium on Physico-chemical Aspects of Dehydrated Protein Rich Milk Products.* Statens Forsogmejeri, Hillerod, Denmark. pp. 160–165

IDF (1991) *Factors Affecting the Yield of Cheese* (Special Issue No. 9301). *IDF, Brussels, Belgium.*

McCrea, I., Harding, F. and Muir, D.D. (1987) Milk compositional quality—opportunities for manipulation. *J. Soc. Dairy Technol.*, **40**(3).

Phelan, J.A. (1981) Standardisation of milk for cheesemaking at factory level. *J. Soc. Dairy Technol.* **34**, 152–156.

Posthumus, G., Booy, C.J. and Klijn, C.J. (1964) The relationship between the protein content of milk and the cheese yield. *Neth. Milk Dairy J.*, **18**, 155–164.

Storry, E.J., Brumby, P.E., Hall, A.J. and Tuckley, B. (1974) Effects of free and protected forms of cod liver oil on milk fat secreation in the dairy cow. *J. Dairy Sci.*, **57**, 1086.

Hygienic quality and animal health

Adams, D.M. (1981) Heat resistant bacterial lipases and ultra-high temperature sterilisation of dairy products. *J. Dairy Sci.*, **64**, 1951–1957.

Barbano, D.M. *et al.* (1991) Influence of milk somatic cell count and milk age on cheese yield. *J. Dairy Sci.*, **74**(2), 369–388.

Coghill, D. and Juffs, H.S. (1979) Incidence of psychrotrophic sporeforming bacteria in pasteurised milk and cream products and effect of temperature growth. *Aus. J. Dairy Technol.*, December, 150–153.

Collins, J. *et al.* (1993) Influence of psychrotrophic bacterial growth in raw milk on the sensory acceptance of UHT skim milk. *J. Food Protection*, **56**(5), 418–425.

Dalgleish, D.G. (1993) Bovine milk protein properties and the manufacturing quality of milk. *Livestock Prod. Sci.*, **35**(1–2), 75–93.

Gillis, W.T. *et al.* (1985) Effects of raw milk quality on ultra-high temperature processed milk. *J. Dairy Sci.*, **68**, 2875–2879.

Grandison, A.S. and Ford, G.D. (1986) Effects of variations in somatic cell count on the rennet coagulation properties and on the yield, composition and quality of Cheddar cheese. *J. Dairy Res.*, **53**(4), 645–655.

IDF (1980) *Flavour Impairment of Milk and Milk Products due to Lipolysis.* (Document 118). IDF, Brussels, Belgium.

Jansen. J.J. (1972) The effect of somatic cell count concentration in the raw milk on shelf life of the processed product. *J. Milk Food Technol.*, **35**(2), 112–114.

Law, B.A. (1979) Enzymes of psychrotrophic bacteria and their effect on milk and milk products. *J. Dairy Res.*, **46**, 573–588.

Meer, R.R. *et al.* (1991) Psychrotrophic *Bacillus* spp. in fluid milk products. A review. *J. Food Protection*, **54**(12), 969–979.

Murphy, S.C. *et al.* (1989) Influence of Bovine mastitis on Lipolysis and proteolysis in milk. *J. Dairy Sci.*, **72**, 620–626.

Needs. E. *et al.* (1988) Influence of somatic cell count on the whipping properties of cream. *J. Dairy Res.*, **55**, 89–95.

Politis, I. and Ng-Kwai-Hang, K.F. (1988) Effects of somatic cell count and milk composition on cheese composition and cheesemaking efficiency. *J. Dairy Sci.*, **71**(7), 1711–1719

Rogers, S.A. (1989) The relationship between somatic cell count, composition and manufacturing properties of bulk milk. 5. Pasteurised milk and skim milk powder. *Aus. J. Dairy Technol.*, **44**(2), 57–60.

Schukker, Y.H. *et al.* (1992) Somatic cell counts and milk quality. *J. Dairy Sci.*, **75**(12), 3352–3358.

Singh, S.P. and Singh, R.S. (1980) Influence of the somatic cell count on the quality of fermented milk. *Ind. J. Dairy Sci.*, **33**(4), 503–505

Westhoff, D. (1981) Microbiology of ultra high temperature milk. *J. Dairy Sci.*, **64**(1).

Westhoff, D. and Dougherty, S.L. (1981) Characterisation of *Bacillus* species isolated from spoiled ultra high temperature processed milk. *J. Dairy Sci.*, **64**, 572–580.

9 Processed milk
F. HARDING

9.1 Introduction

Processing of milk can take many forms. Milk may be consumed as it comes from the cow—raw, heat-treated to kill pathogens and to extend its storage life, frozen, concentrated, with the fat or protein levels modified, with the lactose hydrolysed, homogenised, with cholesterol removed, cultured or with calcium levels enriched. The particular processing used is aimed to produce a modified product in order to meet particular customer demands or a particular niche market.

9.1.1 Raw milk

Milk for direct human consumption is sometimes supplied raw—'as it comes from the cow'. In such a case the milk must be from healthy cows, should be from a bulk supply of low bacterial count and should preferably be bottled and kept cold prior to being consumed. Such milk has a limited demand in developed countries since there is always a risk of diseases such as tuberculosis, brucellosis, salmonellosis, and listeriosis being spread by pathogenic bacteria which are dangerous to human health. Some countries either ban the sale of raw milk for direct human consumption or require it to carry a warning to the effect that such milk may contain bacteria injurious to human health. As a counter argument however, those who support raw milk consumption argue that regular consumption builds up an immunity.

Before heat treatment of milk, milk-borne diseases were once commonplace. Tuberculosis, brucellosis (undulant fever), scarlet fever, diphtheria, typhoid, dysentery and gastroenteritis have all been associated with unhygienic handling of milk. The elimination of these diseases in most countries is generally due to schemes designed to eradicate bovine tuberculosis and brucellosis and to widen consumption of heat-treated milk.

The high likelihood of the presence of pathogens in raw milk has therefore led to the widescale heat treatment of milk. Heat treatment at or above pasteurisation times and temperatures kills all pathogens and most of the spoilage organisms thereby rendering the milk safe to drink as well as extending its shelf-life. More intense heat treatments coupled with aseptic filling are used in order to extend shelf-life of milk further. Milk has also been concentrated, chemically altered and even frozen.

9.1.2 Frozen milk

Pasteurised, homogenised milk packed in polythene bags, providing it is quickly frozen, can be stored in a deep freeze for 12 months or more. This is a means by which fresh milk is often held without deterioration through long sea voyages, etc.

9.1.3 Concentrated milks

Milk may be concentrated by evaporation at low temperatures, under vacuum for subsequent dilution and consumption. Such milks have not, as yet, had significant commercial success although canned evaporated and sweetened condensed milks are widely consumed. In the case of the latter, the milk is first pasteurised then evaporated in steam heated vacuum pans after which it is homogenised, canned and sterilised. These milks, like sterilised milk have a pronounced 'cooked flavour'.

9.1.4 Homogenised milk

Fat in milk is present as discrete globules which, being insoluble and lighter than water, rise to the top in the form of a cream line. This characteristic is used in the commercial separation of cream from milk.

The fat globules in milk vary in size from 1 µm (1/1000 mm) to about 18 µm. The purpose of homogenisation is to uniformly distribute this fat throughout the milk in such a way that it will not separate out. This is achieved by forcing milk through a tiny valve under great pressure. This causes shattering of the fat globules reducing the size to about 1 µm. These small fat globules are naturally stabilised by absorption of casein micelles on the fat globule surface and remain in suspension in the body of the milk.

Homogenised milk is popular in catering establishments since the butterfat remains homogeneous for dispensing. Homogenisation is also essential for long-life milks (sterilised/UHT) since separation of cream in the carton or bottle would make these products unappealing to consumers.

Fat separation or 'creaming' in normal milk keeps any debris such as somatic cells, or small particles of sediment, trapped in the creamline hence preventing their sedimentation. The clarification of milk, a centrifugal separation to remove somatic cells etc., is usual prior to homogenisation otherwise any debris would, in the absence of cream separation, give rise to light brown deposits at the bottom of the bottle of homogenised milk.

When testing for butterfat content in homogenised milk by Gerber it is necessary to spin the butyrometers at least three times after warming to 65°C to ensure that all the fat is recovered.

Several methods exist for the measurement of homogenisation efficiency. The size and range of fat globule in normal milk can be determined microscopically using Sudan Black B dye to colour fat globules. However, spectroturbidimetric methods are better suited to measurement of fat globules in homogenised milks. The simplest test method involves measuring the homogenisation index. The homogenised milk is kept in a measuring cylinder at about 5°C for 48 h after which time the fat content of the top 10% is compared with that of the lower level.

If the fat content of the upper layer is 3.90% and that of the lower layer is 3.70% the homogenisation index is

$$\frac{(3.90 - 3.70) \times 100}{3.90} = 5.1$$

The target index is less than 10 in this very practical and simple test.

9.1.5 Immune milk

A novel niche market has developed for 'Immune Milk'. Milk from cows regularly immunised with a specific vaccine containing sterilised (heat killed) bacteria likely to infect the human gut, induce the cow to produce antibodies to these bacteria which are then secreted into the cow's milk. Humans drinking the milk take in the antibodies hence the milk provides a passive immunity, analogous to the immunity passed from mother to baby with breast milk.

9.2 Heat treatments

9.2.1 Pasteurisation

It was Louis Pasteur in the 1860s who found that wine kept better if it was held at a high temperature for some time then cooled. However, it was not until the early 1900s that similar experiments were undertaken with milk. The object of pasteurisation primarily is to render milk safe, since heat treatment to pasteurisation temperatures and above effectively kills all vegetative organisms dangerous to man. Pasteurisation is defined by the International Dairy Federation (IDF) as "a process applied to a milk product with the object of minimising possible health hazards arising from pathogenic microorganisms associated with milk, by heat treatment which is consistent with minimal chemical, physical and organoleptic change to the product". Without this heat treatment, milk, a perfect growth medium for microorganisms, may well be a source of infection giving rise to diseases such as tuberculosis (*Mycobacterium tuberculosis*), brucellosis (*Brucella abortus*) or food-poisoning from organisms such as *Salmonella* or *Listeria*. To kill pathogenic bacteria minimium combinations of heating times and temperatures are necessary.

Early pasteurisation took the form of a batch process where milk was heated in a large container to 63.5°C for 30 min. In most countries this 'batch' process has been superseded by a technique called HTST (high-temperature–short-time pasteurisation) a continuous flow system in which milk is pumped through a heat exchanger where it is heated to 71.7°C and held at that temperature for 15 s before being rapidly cooled. An upper limit of 65.6°C for the batch process or 80°C for the HTST process is set in order to minimise chemical, physical and organoleptic damage. Thus pasteurised milk should be phosphatase negative since the native enzyme phosphatase is inactivated at 71.7°C/15 s and peroxidase positive since the native enzyme peroxidase is not inactivated until 80°C/15 s is exceeded.

In addition to killing pathogenic microorganisms, pasteurisation also kills most of the spoilage microorganisms which affect the taste and hence limit the shelf-life of milk. There are, however, bacteria which survive HTST heat treatment—these are the thermoduric bacteria which can endure and survive normal heat treatment but are killed by higher temperatures such as sterilisation temperatures.

An improvement in shelf-life of pasteurised milk may be obtained when the milk has been microfiltered to remove thermoduric organisms. Milk which was conventionally pasteurised kept for 6-8 days when stored at 8°C following pasteurisation, whereas after microfiltration the milk had a shelf-life of 16–21 days.

9.2.2   Sterilisation

More severe heat treatment of milk to increase shelf-life has a long history. Sterilisation of milk was practised in the 1880s—even before the homogeniser was invented in 1904. Sterilisation exposes milk to such a high temperature/time combination that effectively all microorganisms are killed. Hence, sterilised milk has an excellent keeping quality (6 months or more at ambient temperatures). This is an advantage particularly in hot climates since sterilised milk can be stored, even at ambient temperatures, for long periods. Whilst sterilised milk is very convenient as it can be stored and used at will, it has the disadvantage of having a distinct 'cooked' caramelised flavour caused by the Maillard reaction leading to a brown discoloration.

Conventional sterilisation is a batch process where milk is clarified to remove somatic cells, etc., homogenised then filled into clean, heated bottles which are hermetically sealed with crown cork caps then placed in a steam chamber. Homogenisation is essential in order to prevent cream rising and forming a plug in the bottle. The sealed capped bottles are then heated to 115–120°C for 15–40 min before being cooled. Sterilisation in this way, after filling and sealing bottles, eliminates the need for aseptic handling of the product. However, the disadvantage is that milk has been exposed to high temperature for a long time and this unfortunately has deleterious effects in that the colour, taste of milk and its vitamin content are all affected.

When milk is kept at a high temperature for a long period of time chemical reactions take place and the resultant reaction products give rise to brown colorisation of milk and a caramel-like flavour. This browning or Maillard reaction is due to chemical combination, under heat, of lactose and milk proteins. These chemicals are used analytically to differentiate sterilised milk from UHT.

9.2.3 UHT treatment

The chemical denaturation of milk quality in sterilised milk has to a large extent, been eliminated—or at best substantially reduced—by UHT treatment. UHT (ultra-high temperature treatment) involves heating milk to 135–150°C for 1–4 s. The advantage of UHT treatment over sterilisation is that, by heating milk to a high temperature for a very short time, one minimises the heat denaturation. Hence, UHT milk has the advantages of sterilised milk in that it has a long shelf-life without the need for refrigeration but is closer in colour and taste to pasteurised milk since the chemical reactions causing the 'cooked' colour and taste in sterilised milk have been minimised by the short time used for heating.

In modern UHT plants, milk is pumped through a closed system during which it is preheated, sterilised, homogenised, cooled, then filled aseptically into sterile containers. Unlike sterilised milk, UHT milk is not heat treated in-container; it is processed in a continuous flow rather than a batch sterilisation system. UHT treatment therefore requires aseptic packaging of the processed milk for the product to have a long safe shelf-life.

UHT milk does, however, still suffer from a degree of heat denaturation. The amount depends on how long it is held at high temperatures, the time taken to reach 135°C and the time taken to cool the heated milk. A process has been patented in which the heat denaturation has been sig-
duced by eliminating heat damage caused during the 'come
l down' period associated with UHT whilst still achieving the
ature for bacterial kill.
that the degree of heat treatment used in milk processing
nt levels of chemical denaturation of milk and these chemical

changes, for example the formation of lactulose, can be measured in order to identify the type of heat treatment which has been used.

9.2.4 Factors affecting the shelf-life of heat-treated milk

The quality of heat-treated milk may be affected by the quality of raw milk from which it is produced (chapter 8), the process control exercised, degree of contamination during the filling stage and, especially in the case of pasteurised milk, temperature control down the chain to the consumer.

The bacteriological quality of the raw milk can affect product quality when psychrotrophic counts are as high as $10^6-10^7/\text{ml}$ since the lipase and protease enzymes produced by the microorganisms may survive heat treatment.

Raw milk may contain one or more of a wide range of pathogens. *Salmonella*, for example, has been shown to be present in raw milk at a rate of greater than 3 in 1000 samples tested. *Listeria* species were present in 15 in 100 samples with 5 in 100 containing *Listeria monocytogenes*.

Pasteurisation kills vegetative pathogens so maintenance of correct pasteurisation conditions and avoidance of post-pasteurisation contamination which could reintroduce pathogens should ensure that milk is safe. For this reason food poisoning outbreaks associated with heat-treated milk are rare. Pathogens (e.g. *Listeria*) can however find access to milk along with other microorganisms between the pasteurisation and filling stage—these are called post-pasteurisation contaminants. Whilst some dairy companies test for pathogens in pasteurised milk, the results of such tests are unlikely to be available until after the milk has been consumed hence the dairy industry relies on good manufacturing practice and HACCP (Hazard Analysis Critical Control Point) systems to ensure that milk is pathogen free.

The major control point in the pasteurised milk chain is the pasteurisation step itself and this is controlled by careful monitoring of thermographs which record the treatment plant time–temperature conditions, the use of flow diversion valves which divert inadequately pasteurised milk back for correct heat treatment and end-product tests. Thus, the phosphatase test is used as a measure of correct heat treatment. The phosphatase test linked with testing for indicator organisms which give a measure of post-pasteurisation contamination by Gram-negative organisms are the key end-product tests for pasteurised milk.

9.3 Quality control of heat-treated milks

9.3.1 Pasteurised milk

Since pasteurised milk has a relatively short shelf-life there is a need for routine quality control of the plant. Thermographs recording pasteurisation time/temperatures should be checked and retained for inspection for at least 6 months. Samples should be taken from the filling line (usually every 0.5 h) to ensure that fat has not separated out in the silo, extraneous water is absent and milk has been correctly pasteurised (phosphatase test). The temperatures of milk held in the cold store prior to distribution should also be checked. This is particularly important with glass bottles of milk where the freshly washed bottle itself may have been warm prior to filling.

The keeping quality of correctly pasteurised milk may be severely reduced by post-pasteurisation contamination (PPC); hence, it is important to check that milk has not been contaminated with Gram-negative bacteria after pasteurisation and prior to bottling or cartoning since very low levels of contamination (1 organism/litre) can ultimately lead to high bacterial numbers if strict temperature control is not practised.

Since it is difficult to measure very low levels of organisms, test methods for PPC involve preincubation to grow bacterial numbers to a measurable level with enumeration being made by one of a number of rapid test methods such as DEFT, ATP or impedance. Selective agents, known to inhibit Gram-positive (thermoduric) bacteria may be added to the sample prior to incubation thus allowing the heat sensitive Gram-negative organisms better conditions for growth.

These test methods not only provide information on PPC but also on potential shelf-life of milk and results can be available within 24–48 h of pasteurisation. The test method defined in EC regulations however requires a 5 day incubation at 6.5°C before counting, resulting in an overall test time of 6 days.

The absence of coliform organisms in milk is sometimes used as an indication of absence of PPC. Whilst the absence of coliforms is a useful guideline test it does not detect as broad a spectrum of organism as does the preincubated tests.

Providing milk has been correctly pasteurised, not recontaminated prior to filling, and held refrigerated, it can be assumed to be pathogen free. However, the number and type of microorganisms entering milk as PPC will be variable. They will certainly include milk spoilage organisms and may occasionally include pathogenic bacteria; much will depend on the type of organisms in the dairy environment. *Listeria monocytogenes*, however, is both a pathogen and a commonly found environmental organism; hence there is a real risk that PPC may introduce Listeria into milk.

From time to time therefore there may be a need to survey milk for the presence of pathogens. *Listeria monocytogenes* is of particular concern since, unlike many other pathogens, it can grow, albeit slowly, at low temperatures particularly in the absence of competing organisms which will have been inhibited by the storage temperatures.

Where pasteurised milk is free from PPC the shelf-life may be restricted by the level of thermoduric organisms in the raw milk if refrigeration is poor. These organisms generally do not grow well at low temperatures; hence minimising their levels in raw milk and adequate cooling of the milk after pasteurisation should ensure a good shelf-life.

9.3.1.1 Measuring the efficiency of heat treatment. Milk being a natural biological fluid contains a wide range of enzymes. Enzymes are naturally occurring proteins which act as specific catalysts. They are best envisaged as a 'key' which unlocks a specific lock or substrate; lactase for example is used by bacteria to 'unlock' the lactose molecule and produce the smaller molecules of glucose and galactose which are more easily digested.

9.3.1.2 The phosphatase test as a measure of correct pasteurisation. In the early 1930s it was noted that a ubiquitous enzyme, alkaline phosphatase (ALP), was present in human blood and its level was related to bone and liver disease in humans. In the time before X-rays and other modern sophisticated techniques this led to an increased interest in ALP measurement.

It was noted that ALP was also a naturally occurring enzyme present in raw milk. Furthermore, it was destroyed by heat at a temperature a few degrees higher than that needed to kill *Mycobacterium tuberculosis*. This time–temperature combination was 63.5°C/30 min; the process is now widely used to provide the minimum high-temperature short-term conditions for pasteurisation (71.7°C/15 s) and gives an equivalent destruction of pathogens and ALP.

Measurement of residual phosphatase, after pasteurisation, therefore offered a means of checking that correct pasteurisation had occurred and that raw milk had not been re-introduced after pasteurisation. The phosphatase test therefore developed as a means of checking the efficient pasteurisation of milk. However, very small quantities of raw milk may contaminate pasteurised milk without causing a failure of the statutary phosphatase test. Contamination by raw milk could result in the re-introduction of pathogens therefore it is important that PPC tests are undertaken regularly.

The basis of the reaction to measure residual phosphatase involves splitting a phosphate radical (H_2PO_4—) from a phosphatase ester R (H_2PO_4) by means of the enzyme phosphatase (Figure 9.1), which is naturally present in milk. The level of phosphatase is different in the milk of different species and this needs to be taken into account when interpreting the test (chapter 7).

Since its first use in the early 1930s the test has undergone a number of modifications in order to improve the speed of test or its sensitivity by

$$R-O-\overset{\overset{\displaystyle O}{\|}}{\underset{\underset{\displaystyle OH}{|}}{P}}-OH + H_2O \longrightarrow R-OH + H_3PO_4$$

Figure 9.1   The principle of the alkaline phosphatase test.

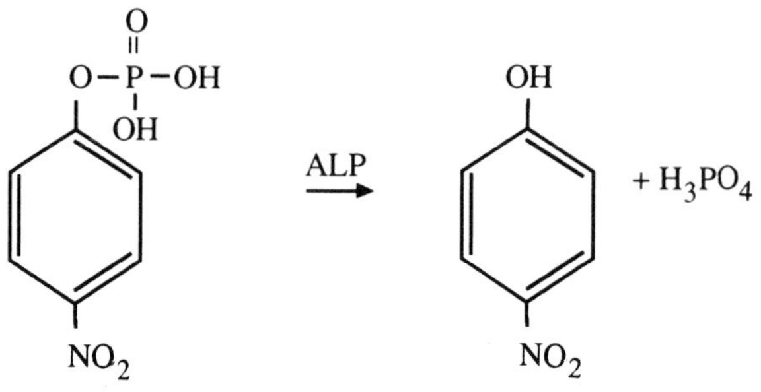

p - Nitrophenylphosphate   p - Nitrophenol

Figure 9.2   Phosphatase test based on liberation of p-nitrophenol.

changing the substrate and hence the reagent (R) released by the reaction of the enzyme. Originally, phenyl phosphate was used with the liberated phenol being measured by means of coupling it with a colour reagent to produce an indophenol. The test involves a 24 h incubation for quantitative determination. It is important with this substrate that sources of external 'free' phenol from rubber bungs, etc., are eliminated.

p-Nitrophenylphosphate was later introduced (Figure 9.2) as the substrate to be measured since the release of p-nitrophenol gave a visible yellow colour which can be measured in alkaline solution and quantified at 405 nm.

A further development involved the use of a phenolphthalein phosphate substrate; in the presence of ALP this freed phenolphthalein which when liberated gave a red colour in alkaline solution, the absorbance of which could be measured spectrophotometrically at 540 nm. This method, however, seems not to have found favour commercially.

These methods are used for statutory control of pasteurisation but they are relatively slow and laborious for the operator since they involve a series of steps to clarify milk prior to measurement. Also they are relatively insensitive, measuring down to only 0.1% raw milk in pasteurised milk and are limited in that they cannot be used for milk products which

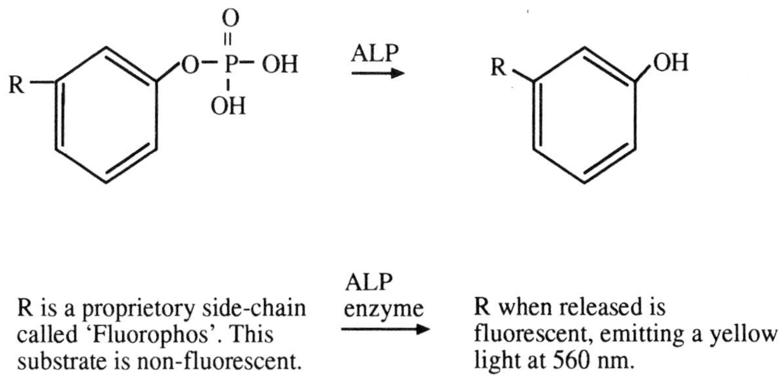

R is a proprietary side-chain
called 'Fluorophos'. This
substrate is non-fluorescent.

ALP
enzyme
⟶

R when released is
fluorescent, emitting a yellow
light at 560 nm.

Figure 9.3 Principle of the Fluorophos ALP test.

are coloured. A number of standards describing methods of test have been published by ISO, AOAC and IDF.

A new method has been recently developed by Advanced Instruments in the USA (Rocco) and involves the use of a proprietory substrate as the phosphate monoester (Figure 9.3). This proprietory substrate is not of itself fluorescent, however, the liberated phenol derivative, the concentration of which is directly related to the amount of the ALP enzyme present in milk is highly fluorescent and can be measured at low levels.

This new technique (Fluorophos) has a number of distinct advantages over the traditional methods, being nearly 20 times more sensitive, requiring few manipulations by the operator, being quicker (3 min) and, using a fluorometric rather than a colorimetric method, it can also be used for coloured products such as flavoured milks, egg nogs, cheese and many other milk products.

9.3.1.2.1 Interpretation of test results. The three methods used most widely to determine residual phosphatase are based on different substrates.

(a) The Aschaffenburg and Mullen (1949) method: in this method *p*-nitrophenol is liberated and is measured colorimetrically (IDF Standard 82A: 1987—Milk and dried milk, buttermilk and buttermilk powder, whey and whey powder). This reference method describes a method based on the liberation and measurement of *p*-nitrophenol.

(b) The Scharer (1938) method: in this method phenol is liberated and is measured colorimetrically (IDF Standard 63; 1971—Milk and milk powder, buttermilk and buttermilk powder, whey and whey powder—determination of phosphatase activity (reference method)).

(c) The Fluorophos method in which a Fluorometric substrate is liberated (ISO/DIS Standard 11816: 1995—Milk and milk based drinks—determination of alkaline phosphatase activity (fluorimetric method) describes the Fluorometric method)

The fact that there are three methods giving different end-products of measurement clearly creates problems with cross correlation of methods. The stautory maximum residual phosphatase activity in properly pasteurised milk is 10 µg/ml for the *p*-nitrophenol method and 1.0 µg/ml for the phenol-based test. The equivalent value for the Fluorophos technique is 500 milliunits (mu)/litre. At these maximum values, test methods measure about 0.1–0.2% raw milk in properly pasteurised milk. This level of detection was established historically in the 1930s and 1940s simply because this was the lowest level of detection capable of being met by the colorimetric methods then available.

The more recently developed fluorometric technique however will measure as little as 15–30 mu/litre and this is equivalent to 0.003–0.006% raw milk in pasteurised milk. In time this may lead to a tightening of the statutory maximum raw milk allowed in pasteurised milk since this would reduce further the risk of pathogens from raw milk being carried into the pasteurised product. The Fluorophos, being a fluorometric measurement, can, unlike colorimetric methods, be used for direct determination of ALP in coloured products such as flavoured milks.

Presently, it offers the dairy industry a very important and effective quality control tool for monitoring pasteurisation plants. By measuring the residual phosphatase between the minimum detection limit (say 30 mu/litre) and the statutory maximum of 500 one can produce a continuous picture of the status of pasteuriser plates. Any leakage of plates will cause an increase in the residual phosphatase as raw milk levels increase even though the statutory level may not be breached.

Further uncertainty as to the interpretation of how much raw milk equates to a specific residual phosphatase level is created by the fact that the initial pool of phosphatase in cow's milk can vary. Whilst on average the pool for cow's milk is about 3500 µg phenol/ml (where the statutory maximum value of 1.0 µg would equate to about 0.03% raw milk), the range reported is very wide (1870–4740 µg). For this reason it is normally recommended that 0.1 ml of the fresh raw milk to be pasteurised is added to 100 ml of milk laboratory heat-treated to 95°C for 1 min. This gives a positive control of 0.1% raw milk against which the commercially pasteurised milk can be judged.

The interpretation of the test is different again for sheep's and goat's milk since the initial pool of ALP is very different from cow's milk. Raw sheep's milk has a much higher pool of ALP (8300–16 300 μg phenol/ml) than cow's milk (1870–4700) and raw goat's milk has a much lower pool (117–1292). It is therefore especially important when applying the test to sheep or goat milk to take a sample of the raw milk prior to pasteurisation and make a control sample against which to judge the commercial sample.

If one assumes that the average native ALP in goat milk is 700 μg phenol/ml then the colorimetric methods will be able to measure about 0.15–0.2% raw milk. At the lower end of the variation however, with a starting value of 117 μg phenol/ml, colorimetric methods would only detect about 0.9% raw milk. This is not sensitive enough and the Fluorophos technique would provide a much more sensitive control. The limit currently set for well-pasteurised goat's milk is 0.67 μg phenol/ml. The bacteriological count of goat milk, especially where hand milking is practised, can be much higher than that of cow's milk making the possibility of heat stable microbial phosphatase more likely.

Care also needs to be taken in the interpretation of the test where milk has received a previous heat treatment. For example, where pasteurised skim-milk is blended with raw whole milk in the production of low fat (e.g. semi-skimmed milk) the pool of phosphatase mixture will have been reduced and the test sensitivity lowered.

9.3.1.2.2 Measuring ALP in cheese. There is sometimes a need to be able to ascertain whether a cheese has been made from raw or pasteurised milk. In some countries this differentiation is required because raw milk cheeses carry an 'added value'. On the other hand raw milk cheeses may be considered a greater health risk by virtue of them carrying pathogens into cheese from the raw milk. Measurement of residual ALP in the cheese provides the means of this assessment. The Fluorophos method has been used for this measurement. Variation in the natural pool of phosphatase, variation in the milk solids of differing cheeses and partitioning of the ALP, variation in the microbial phosphatase and the potential for reactivated phosphatase all make it difficult to set a universal maximum residual ALP for cheese. Data has therefore to be built up for specific cheeses. Work has been undertaken on ALP measurement in the Netherlands and in Germany which demonstrate that the Fluorophos method can be used effectively for cheeses.

9.3.1.2.3 Partitioning of ALP. Phosphatase is readily absorbed on fat globules hence cream and high-fat products contain more ALP than skim-milk and low-fat products. For example, whereas wholemilk has an ALP pool of about 3500 μg phenol/ml, skim-milk has about half and heavy cream four times the pool present in whole milk.

9.3.1.2.4 Reactivation of phosphatase. Positive residual phosphatase is normally an indication of incorrect pasteurisation or recontamination by unpasteurised milk; however, there is a need to check for false positives.

Under certain conditions phosphatase inactivated by correct pasteurisation may reappear. This tends to be more prevalent in high fat products such as cream stored at temperatures over 20°C. Reactivated phosphatase can be differentiated from residual phosphatase by incubation of the sample in the presence of magnesium ions.

9.3.1.2.5 Heat-stable microbial phosphatase. Certain bacteria are known to produce heat-stable microbial phosphatase. If milk is stored for long periods of time prior to pasteurisation, psychrotrophic bacteria can grow and produce heat-stable ALP which could yield a positive phosphatase test. Where positive ALP tests occur therefore it is recommended that the test is repeated on a laboratory pasteurised sample in order to judge whether the failure is genuinely due to residual, heat labile ALP or due to heat stable microbial phosphatase.

9.3.1.2.6 Practical application of the test. The ALP test has until recently been used as a pass or fail test for efficient pasteurisation. The development of the new, much more sensitive Fluorophos technique enables the test to be used to monitor the efficiency of pasteuriser plant operation. Operating under the minimum time–temperature conditions (71.7°C/15 s) the residual ALP level should be monitored regularly. If it increases significantly, even though it does not rise sufficiently to fail the statutory test, the cause may be

(a) a drop in pasteurisation temperatures,
(b) an ingress of raw milk—perhaps from pinholes in the heat exchanger plates, or
(c) increased levels of heat-stable microbial phosphatase.

ALP levels increasing above the normally expected background level for that plant should be investigated as part of a good manufacturing regime. The native enzyme peroxidase in milk is inactivated by heating milk to 80°C and the test for peroxidase is used to check that pasteurised milk has not been overheated.

9.3.1.3 Tests for post-pasteurisation contamination (PPC). The phosphatase test is used to demonstrate that pasteurised milk has been heated to the correct time–temperature conditions (72°C/15 s) and that raw milk has not been remixed with the pasteurised product. However, it is also important for the processor to be assured that milk has been bottled or cartoned with the minimum level of bacterial recontamination. This can of course be achieved by aseptic filling. However, this is expensive and is not generally practised for normal retail milks other than UHT.

The shelf-life of pasteurised milk contaminated prior to packaging may be as little as a few days if stored at 8°C compared with 21 days or more for uncontaminated milk. Even longer storage times are reported for lower chill storage temperatures (0–4°C).

Gram-negative bacteria such as coliforms are killed by pasteurisation and these are therefore used as the indicator organisms for PPC.

9.3.1.4 Total count. The total count of pasteurised milk has been considered as a quality control test. However, since plates are incubated at 30°C for 72 h this test would also count thermoduric organisms; hence this test is not suitable for specifically assessing contaminating organisms. Thermoduric organisms are less of a threat to the keeping quality of pasteurised milk since their growth rate at low temperature is much less than that of psychrotrophs and many species do not grow at all.

9.3.1.5 Gram-negative organisms.

9.3.1.5.1 Coliform test. Coliforms are Gram-negative organisms which do not survive pasteurisation and are contaminants associated with poor hygiene. Their presence in milk is an indication of PPC and is ascertained using selective media based on lactose fermentation and resistance to bile salts.

The coliform test is of value as a measure of PPC where the presence of coliform contaminants is likely; it is, however, a less reliable indicator since the contaminating Gram-negative flora may be free from coliforms.

9.3.1.5.2 Pseudomonads. Since very low levels of the contaminants (as low as 1 per litre) may significantly adversely affect the keeping quality of pasteurised milk, to enumerate them it is necessary to preincubate samples under test, either in the retail container or in the form of a subsample, in order to increase bacterial numbers to measurable levels prior to test. Preincubation in the retail package ensures that samples are not accidentally contaminated during the subsampling stage. However, the disadvantage is that it creates the need for large incubation units to house the large volume of milk being incubated.

At the end of the preincubation stage the bacteria which have grown can be enumerated by traditional plating techniques or rapid bacterial testing methods discussed earlier.

Inhibition of heat resistant Gram-positive organisms can be achieved by using a mixture of crystal violet, penicillin and Nisin which is designed to ensure that any organisms counted are truly PPC.

9.3.1.5.3 Cytochrome oxidase test. Gram-negative psychrotrophs are normally killed by pasteurisation; hence their presence in pasteurised milk is a measure of PPC which affects the shelf-life. These bacteria possess the cytochrome oxidase system hence colorimetric measurement of the enzyme cytochrome oxidase has been considered as a means of predicting the shelf-life of pasteurised milk.

The method is rapid, cheap and simple as a means of monitoring trends in the hygiene of pasteurised milk production. However, the test is prone to false positives and false negatives making it unreliable as a 'one off' test.

9.3.1.6 The future. Fourier-transform infrared spectroscopy (FTIR) is believed to offer a method for the future for special fingerprinting of intact bacteria. The infrared patterns recorded comprise the vibrational characteristics of the DNA/RNA cell constituents and cell wall components.

DNA and ribosomal RNA probes are being produced for specific identification of organisms.

9.3.1.7 Measurement of the microbiological history of milk. Since vegetative microorganisms are killed by heat treatment and their cells may be broken down in the processing of milk, attempts to measure the microbial status of the raw milk using microbial cell counting techniques would prove futile. However, an indication of the hygienic history of a product can be obtained by measurement of Gram-negative bacterial lipopolysaccharides (LPS) in the processed milk or milk product.

Gram-negative bacteria are indicators of production hygiene and they produce LPS, a high-molecular-weight heat stable complex, which is a component of the Gram-negative cell wall. Thus, the level of LPS in milk or milk products gives a measure of the Gram-negative bacteria originally present. As the component is heat stable, it provides a measure of live and dead cells.

LPS is measured by a blood clotting mechanism from the Florida horseshoe crab (*Limulus polyphemus*). A lysate of amoebocyte cells from *Limulus polyphemus* gels in the presence of LPS. Using end-point titration the presence or absence of a gel is used to quantify the level of LPS present in the sample. The test is now commercially available, can measure extremely low levels (10–15 μg) of LPS per ml and can be used to indicate the microbiological history of pasteurised, UHT and sterilised milks.

9.3.2 UHT milk

The bacterial quality of raw milk, providing it is of a reasonably good quality, should not be a limiting factor in the production of UHT milk. Milk with a very high bacterial count ($>10^6$ psychrotrophs/ml) however may give rise to the occurrence of heat resistant enzymes produced mainly by *Pseudomonas fluorescens* which themselves are killed in the heating process. Heat-stable proteases affect the stability of milk during the UHT treatment and during subsequent storage. These can give rise to off-flavours and gelation in UHT milk during ambient storage for several months. There is also a risk of heat-resistant lipases developing; hence UHT milk should not normally be produced from raw milk which has been stored at low temperature for prolonged periods (chapter 8).

A rapid and sensitive method is being developed for protease assay using a modification of the bioluminescence technique. The principle of the test is that luciferase catalyses the reaction of ATP and luciferin to produce light—the reaction originates from fireflies. ATP is found in all living cells and supplies the source of energy to power biological reactions. Psychrotrophic protease is incubated in the presence of luciferase, an enzyme, which degrades and causes a light output when luciferin and ATP are added. This rapid (5 min) method for the determination of low levels of protease is now available in kit form.

Aseptic filling is an essential part of the UHT process and to ensure that sterility has been achieved a proportion of containers is often stored at 30°C for 15 days followed by a standard plate count. Indirect but more rapid methods may also be used after preincubation. The aseptic failure rate should preferably be lower than 1 in 100 000 and certainly not higher than 1 in 10 000 and therefore extremely high random sampling rates (>300 per run) are required. However, it is statistically unlikely that a practical sampling schedule would be capable of detecting anything other than a major spoilage rate.

All quality control sampling regimes assume that careful records of sampling times and plant records have been kept in order to help retrospective searches identify the cause of any product failures.

9.3.3 Sterilised milk

Milk will have been heat treated, clarified and homogenised before being filled in the container in which it is to be sold, when, after sealing the container, the second stage sterilisation heating takes place. This second heating of the sealed container is a very severe process which should render the product sterile. This does not infer that poor quality raw milk can be used since, as with UHT milk products, it is important that raw milk is of a reasonable bacteriological quality.

Sterilised milk is usually checked using the Aschaffenburg turbidity test which is a measure that milk has had the correct time–temperature heat treatment. This test involves precipitation of casein and heat denatured whey protein from milk. In the case of sterilised milk a test for residual non-heat denatured whey protein would prove negative whereas UHT milk will give a positive test for whey protein since they will not have been totally denatured by the less severe UHT heat treatment.

9.4   Milks of modified compositional quality

The liquid milk market in many countries has become very sophisticated in recent years as the dairy industry has developed a range of milks of modified compositional quality to meet varying dietary requirements. The most usual compositional manipulation is that of fat content.

9.4.1   Fat-reduced milks

The fat content of 'normal' milk varies from breed to breed, season to season and country to country. In many countries the natural fat level is about 4%. To meet the requirement of people who wish to reduce the amount of fat in their diet the sale of reduced fat milks has grown considerably. Standards set vary from country to country but the usual levels chosen are skim (up to 0.3%), semi-skimmed 1.5–1.8% fat and standardised whole milk 3.5% fat. These milks are usually produced by reducing the fat in milk by centrifugation in a commercial separator. This can produce milk with virtually no (less than 0.1%) fat and high-fat cream which is usually sold as cream or made into butter. The skim-milk fraction may also be spray dried or blended with whole milk in order to reduce its fat content to the desired level.

The blending process for semi-skimmed or standardised milk can be achieved in a batch process where a silo of milk is standardised prior to heat treatment but is more usually achieved in a continuous flow system whereby the fat content of the blend of milk from two silos (one containing whole milk and one containing skim) is continuously tested by an instrumental method (chapter 6).There is also a move in some countries to standardise the protein content of consumer milk.

Skim-milk is perceived by consumers to have a poor body and flavour compared with semi-skimmed or whole milk. Microcrystalline cellulose and sodium carboxymethylcellulose have been used as additives to skimmed milk to increase the viscosity from about 7 to 90–120 centipoise when the milk is allowed to stand, and 30–60 when it is stirred or poured. This additive mixture also improves mouthfeel making skim-milk taste more like whole milk. Similar improvements in mouthfeel and viscosity can be achieved by adding non-fat milk solids but this also increases the calorific value to about 120–130 compared with 80–90 for skim-milk.

9.4.2 Lactose-reduced milks

Human beings require the enzyme lactase in order to break lactose into its constituent parts, glucose and galactose, for digestion. Not all humans have lactase hence a market has developed for lactose-reduced milks. Lactose reduction can be achieved by careful dosing of UHT milk cartons with the enzyme lactase after the UHT heat treatment and during packaging. Lactose is about 90% hydrolysed after 10 days storage at room temperature (20°C). The cost of the enzyme is minimal; however, greater control over the rate of hydrolysis is achieved when using immobilised lactase, where the enzyme is locked onto a column over which the milk is passed. Quality control of the degree of hydrolysis is achieved by measurement of residual lactose.

9.5 Compositional quality of fluid milk products

The gross compositional quality (fat, protein and lactose) and the water soluble mineral content of milks and creams will depend on the proportion of fat and serum in the product. Table 9.1 gives the variation of constituents per 100 g of product for a range of milks. The vitamin content will vary according to whether the vitamin is fat-soluble or water soluble. Vitamins A, D and E, for example, are fat-soluble hence decrease in low-fat milks. This is why in some countries vitamin supplementation of low-fat milks is common practice.

Table 9.2 gives similar figures for creams and butter where not only the variation in fat-soluble and serum-soluble vitamins is more pronounced but the mineral levels associated with the serum fraction show a more significant variation.

A number of vitamins, vitamin A, C and riboflavin, for example, are also sensitive to sunlight and will be reduced if exposed to light. Others, thiamin, vitamins B_1, B_{12} and C are diminished by processing and their levels will depend on the processing history of the product.

Table 9.1 Variation in quality criteria for a range of milks: Constituents per 100 g[a]

	CI[b]	Whole	Semi-skimmed	Skim	Unfortified skim powder	Evaporated full cream
Energy (kJ)	320	276	194	140	1491	664
Protein (g)	3.6	3.2	3.3	3.3	36	8.2
Carbohydrates (g)	4.6	4.6	4.7	4.8	50.1	12
Fat (g)	4.9	3.9	1.6	0.1	1.0	9
Saturates (g)	3.1	2.5	1.0	0.06	0.6	5.8
Mono (g)	1.1	1.0	0.4	Trace	0.2	2.1
Poly (g)	0.1	0.1	0.1	Trace	Trace	0.2
Trans (g)	0.3	0.2	0.1	Trace	Trace	0.5
Vitamins						
A (µg)	60	52	25	Trace	Trace	80
Thiamin (mg)	0.04	0.04	0.04	0.04	0.38	0.06
Riboflavin (mg)	0.19	0.17	0.18	0.18	1.6	0.42
Nicotinic acid (mg)	0.08	0.08	0.09	0.1	1.0	0.25
B_6 (mg)	0.06	0.06	0.06	0.06	0.6	0.07
Folic acid (µg)	5	5	5	5	50	11
B_{12} (µg)	0.3	0.4	0.4	0.4	2.5	0.1
Pantothenic acid (mg)	0.3	0.3	0.3	0.3	3.3	0.8
Biotin (µg)	2	2	2	2	20	4
C (mg)	1.5	1.5	1.5	1.5	13	1.5
D (µg)	0.04	0.03	0.01	Trace	Trace	0.09
E (mg)	0.1	0.08	0.03	Trace	Trace	0.6
Minerals						
Sodium (g)	0.05	0.06	0.06	0.06	0.56	0.19
Calcium (mg)	130	115	118	120	1250	310
Chloride (mg)	80	100	100	100	1080	250
Copper (µg)	3	3	3	3	0.2	0.1
Iodine (µg)	30	30	30	30	300	NA
Iron (mg)	0.05	0.05	0.05	0.05	0.4	0.2
Magnesium (mg)	12	11	11	12	130	30
Phosphorus (mg)	100	90	95	95	970	250
Potassium (mg)	120	130	130	140	1580	350
Selenium (µg)	2	2	2	2	20	NA
Zinc (mg)	0.4	0.4	0.4	0.4	4	1

[a]Source: England and Wales National Dairy Council booklet '*Composition of standard UK dairy products*'.
[b]CI, Channel Island (i.e. Jersey/Guernsey milk).

Table 9.2 Variation of quality criteria for a range of creams and butter: Constituents per 100 g[a]

	Half (12%fat)	Single (18%fat)	Whipping (40%fat)	Double (48%fat)	Sterilised (23%fat)	Butter (2%added)
Energy (kJ)	573	776	1564	1849	957	3014
Protein (g)	2.9	2.6	2.0	1.7	2.6	0.5
Carbohydrates (g)	4.1	3.9	3.0	2.6	3.7	0.5
Fat (g)	12.3	18.0	40.0	48.0	23.0	81
Saturates (g)	7.9	11.5	25.6	30.7	14.7	51.8
Mono (g)	2.9	4.2	9.4	11.2	5.4	18.9
Poly (g)	0.2	0.4	0.8	0.9	0.5	1.6
Trans (g)	0.7	1.0	2.3	2.7	1.3	4.6
Vitamins						
A (µg)	130	190	350	430	200	830
Thiamin (mg)	0.03	0.04	0.02	0.02	0.03	Trace
Riboflavin (mg)	0.17	0.16	0.16	0.16	0.16	Trace
Nicotinic acid (mg)	0.07	0.07	0.04	0.04	0.06	Trace
B_6 (mg)	0.05	0.04	0.04	0.03	0.02	Trace
Folic acid (µg)	6	6	6	6	1	Trace
B_{12} (µg)	0.2	0.2	0.2	0.2	<0.1	Trace
Pantothenic acid (mg)	0.3	0.3	0.2	0.2	0.25	Trace
Biotin (µg)	1.7	1.8	1.4	1	2	Trace
C (mg)	0.8	0.8	0.7	0.6	0.03	Trace
D (µg)	0.08	0.12	0.23	0.28	0.14	0.76
E (mg)	0.4	0.4	0.8	1.0	0.5	2
Minerals						
Sodium (g)	0.05	0.05	0.04	0.04	0.05	0.79
Calcium (mg)	100	90	60	50	90	15
Chloride (mg)	90	80	60	50	75	1210
Copper (mg)	<0.1	<0.1	<0.1	<0.1	<0.2	0.03
Iodine (µg)	<20	<20	<20	<20	<20	NA
Iron (mg)	0.3	0.3	0.2	0.2	0.3	0.2
Magnesium (mg)	11	9	7	6	11	2
Phosphorus (mg)	80	75	60	50	78	25
Potassium (mg)	125	120	80	65	110	15
Zinc (mg)	0.3	0.3	0.2	0.2	0.2	0.2

[a]Source: England and Wales National Dairy Council booklet 'Composition of standard UK dairy products'.

References and further reading

Aschaffenburg, R. and Mullen, J.E.C. (1949) A rapid and simple phosphatase test for milk. *J Dairy Res.*, **16**, 58–67.

Anon (1985) Keeping quality of pasteurised milk. *Dairy Industry*, **30**(1), 46–50.

Anon (1992) Prevention is the best medicine for pasteurisation tests. *Dairy Foods*, **May**.

Anon (1993) Boosting milks appeal. *Dairy Foods*, **Feb**, 56.

Birar Roseira, M.L. de and Barbosa, M. (1995) Phosphatase activity levels in pasteurised goat's milk. *J. Soc. Dairy Technol.*, **48**(1), 9–12.

Harding, F., Morris, J.L. and Fryatt, R. (1975) The effect of somatic cells on the reference method for the determination of dirt in milk. *J. Assoc. Public Anal.*, **13**, 125–132.

IDF (1981) *Factors Affecting the Keeping Quality of Heat Treated Milk* (Bulletin Doc. 130). IDF, Brussels, Belgium.

IDF (1983) *Heat Resistant Proteinases in UHT Products* (Bulletin Doc. 157). IDF, Brussels, Belgium.

IDF (1986) *Monograph on Pasteurised Milk* (Bulletin 200). IDF, Brussels, Belgium.

IDF (1988) Listeria monocytogenes *in Food. Its significance and Methods for its Detection* (Bulletin 223). IDF, Brussels, Belgium.

IDF (1989) *Monograph on Heat-Induced Changes in Milk.* (Bulletin No. 238). IDF, Brussels, Belgium.

IDF (1991) *Alkaline Phosphatase Test as a Measure of Correct Pasteurisation* (Bulletin 262). IDF, Brussels, Belgium.

IDF (1992) *Pasteurisation of Cream* (Bulletin 271). IDF, Brussels, Belgium.

Kay, H.D. and Graham, W.R. (1935) The phosphatase test for pasteurised milk. *J. Dairy Res.*, **6**, 191–203.

Kosikowski, F. (1988) Enzyme behaviour and utilisation in dairy technology. *J. Dairy Sci.*, **71**, 557–573.

O'Donnell, E.T. (1995) The incidence of *Salmonella* and *Listeria* in raw milk from bulk tanks in England and Wales. **48**(1), 25–29.

Rocco, R.M. (1990) Fluorometric analysis of alkaline phosphatase in fluid dairy products. *J Food Protection*, **53**(7), 588–591.

Scharer, H. (1938) A rapid phosphomonesterase test for control of dairy pasteurisation. *J. Dairy Sci.*, **21**, 21–34.

Wright, R.C. and Tramer, J.J. (1953) *Dairy Res.*, **2**, 177.

10 Contaminants

W. HEESCHEN and F. HARDING

10.1 Intoduction

There are conflicting pressures on dairy farmers. Milk should be clean and yet free from traces of detergents. Milk should be from healthy cows, yet should not contain residues of antibiotics. Additionally, as analytical methods have become ever more sensitive the farmers' ability to meet a zero tolerance for residues of contaminants has become ever more difficult.

The balance is being addressed in a pragmatic way by the setting of maximum levels which focus on safe upper limits or, where human health is not at risk, maximum levels which should not be exceeded if good agricultural practice is followed. Good agricultural practice (GAP) simply aims to minimise contaminant residues, such as pesticides, in food by requiring that minimum quantities needed to achieve adequate control are used. This therefore aims to guard against excessive or careless application of pesticides, etc.

Based on what might be expected to find access to food under GAP applications of a pesticide, for example, authorities set maximum residue limits (MRLs) in milk. The MRL is the level of the contaminant which should not be exceeded, providing the pesticide has been correctly and sensibly applied, and sets standards against which prosecutions can be brought.

When there is a human health threat for a residue, then maximum acceptable limits are set using acceptable daily intake (ADI) values. The ADI is an ultra-safe maximum limit in that it sets the standard against which the chemical can be consumed for an entire lifetime without risk to the health of the consumer. If there is uncertainty about the affects of a chemical, temporary ADI values are set until the uncertainty is resolved.

There is therefore an upper limit of acceptance or a maximum residue limit set for most potential residues. At the extreme, for highly toxic materials, this is a zero tolerance—where no measurable amount of the substance is acceptable. Where the chemical is 'dose dependent' on humans, ADI values are set at very safe levels and where no toxicological data is available MRLs are set to ensure that chemical abuse does not give rise to unnecessarily high levels of residues in foods.

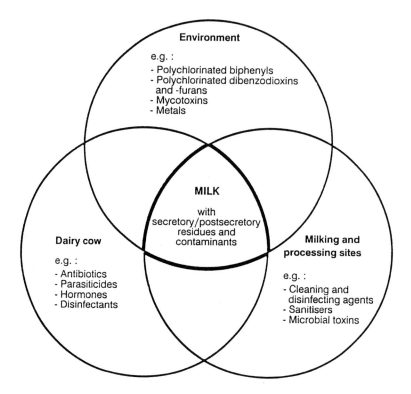

Figure 10.1   Residues and contaminants in milk and milk products.

Against such standards the dairy industry is able to judge its performance and bearing in mind that milk is a natural unrefined foodstuff milk stands up well to the in-depth analysis it is subjected to.

Milk is at risk of being contaminated from a wide variety of chemical residues (Figure 10.1) introduced via treatment of the cow, her feed, the milking environment and the processing plant and there is therefore a need to minimise the risk of contamination in each area by adopting sensible control measures. Potential chemical contaminants are

- Antibiotics
- Hormones

- Disinfectants
- Nitrites, nitrates and nitrosamines
- Pesticides
- PCBs
- Mycotoxins
- Toxic metals
- Dioxins

10.2 Veterinary drugs

10.2.1 Importance of drugs

Antibiotics are used on dairy cattle to help control disease. The most usual treatment is intramammary infusion into an inflamed quarter for treatment of mastitis. The drug is infused using a syringe-like application. The length of time the drug is retained in the udder is controlled by the base in which it is dispersed. Antibiotics dispersed in oil-based solvents are retained in the udder longer than those in water-based solvents and drug companies set the 'retention' time for their preparations by trials involving milking cows. Once the upper limit of the antibiotic acceptability—the MRL—is set, the drug manufacturer normally has to satisfy licensing authorities that, providing farmers follow the withholding time on the preparation, they will not fail to meet the MRL for the bulk supply.

Antibiotic residues are undesirable in milk. It is argued that regular ingestion of antibiotics may encourage the development of antibiotic-resistant strains of organisms in man and may lead to failure to respond to therapeutic doses of antibiotic at a later stage. Some people are also highly sensitive to antibiotics. Penicillin allergy, for example, could be triggered by trace levels in food. Antibiotics not only inhibit or kill disease organisms in man but also inhibit the bacteria used to produce cheese and yogurt, therefore antibiotic residues pose not only problems in human health but also a threat to the quality of manufactured products (Table 10.1)

10.2.2 Test methods

Test methods must have a sensitivity which meets the MRLs for consumer protection as well as those required to protect starter cultures. The most widely used methods are microbial inhibitor tests. These methods, as the name describes, involve growth of specific test organisms such as *Bacillus stearothermophilus* being inhibited if an antibiotic is present in milk. The test organism is cultured in a small well in the presence of nutrients and

Table 10.1 Sensitivity of microorganisms of importance in dairy technology (e.g. Yogurt cultures) and the test organism, *Bacillus stearothermophilus*, to antibiotics

Culture	Penicillin (IU/ml)	Streptomycin (µg/ml)	Chlor-amphenicol (mg/ml)	Chlortetra-cycline (mg/ml)	Oxytetra-cycline (mg/ml)
Streptococcus thermophilus	0.0017–0.17	0.5–5.0	0.05–0.1	0.001–0.01	0.001–0.01
Streptococcus cremoris	0.05–0.1	—	—	—	—
Lactobacillus bulgaricus	0.3–0.6	—	0.3–5.0	—	—
Butter starter	0.017–0.17	0.1–0.2	0.1–0.2	0.01–0.1	0.01–0.1
Cheese starter	0.05–0.2	0.04	0.04	0.02–0.25	0.01
Bacillus stearothermophilus var. <u>calidolactis</u>	0.001–0.008	0.6–1	1	0.6–1	1

an indicator dye. Under normal conditions the culture grows and the dye colour is changed from blue to yellow. If an antibiotic is present the culture is killed and the dye remains blue. Such test methods are generally used as screening tests and samples found to be positive are retested. Whilst sensitive to a range of antibiotics, the test organism most widely used is generally more sensitive to penicillin than to other antibiotics. Modification of the pH of the test organism can however change the test sensitivity to different antibiotics.

Bacterial inhibition tests tend to be lengthy (3 h) and as a result tend to be used for penalising farmers after the milk has been processed. There is now a growing interest in more rapid tests which take less than 10 min to perform and can be used to reject milk prior to processing thereby mini-mising the risk of contaminated milk reaching the consumer. These rapid tests, termed competitive immunoassays, use highly specific antibodies to detect antibiotic residues in raw milk. These test kits can detect as little as 1 ppb (1 ng/ml) of antibiotic in milk and can be performed in about 10–15 min. They do not require highly skilled technicians to perform the ana-lyses. The use of financial penalties based on microbial inhibition tests has however proved to be successful in most countries. In the UK, for example, the incidence of antibiotics in milk in the early 1990s was one-fortieth that found in the 1960s. This dramatic reduction was achieved because farmers failing the test suffered a very severe penalty equating to almost the full value of the milk being consigned.

Until recently an MRL has been set for penicillin without specified limits being given for other antibiotics. This is now changing with MRLs now having been set for a wide range of antibiotics (Table 10.2) for which appropriate test methods are being developed.

Table 10.2 Antibiotics maximum residue limits (MRL)[a]

Antibiotic	MRL (ppb)
Benzyl penicillin	4.0
Ampicillin	4
Amoxicillin	4
Oxacillin	30
Cloxacillin	30
Dicloxacillin	30
Sulphonamides	100
Trimethoprim	50
Dapsone	25
Tetracyclines	100
Spiramycin	150
Febantel	10
Fenbendazole	10
Oxfendazole	10
Levamisol	10
Tylosin	50
Albendazole	100
Thiabendazole	100

[a]Source: EC Directives 2377/90, 675/92 and 3093/92.

10.3 Keeping antibiotics out of milk

Dairy farmers are usually well aware of the reasons why it is necessary to keep antibiotics out of milk and of the risk of heavy penalties or even prosecution if they fail to do so. Not all, however, develop milking regimes aimed at minimising the risk of contaminating the supply they send to market. Providing they follow a good regime, farmers should have no fear of failing the test.

10.3.1 Correct and clear identification of treated cows

It is essential that the milker knows exactly which cows have been treated so that he can take care with that milk. Freeze branding or some other permanent identification of the cow is necessary together with a more temporary means (tail tag, udder dye) of showing which cows have been drug treated.

10.3.2 Record all treatments

It is the law in some countries that all treatments of the cow should be recorded as a permanent written record. This should include the identity of the cow, the person giving the antibiotic treatment, type of treatment, dosage given, date and time (or milking) of treatment and the milking at which the prescribed withholding time ends and the milk can safely be included for sale. Cows bought in to the herd should also be checked before their milk is included for sale.

10.3.3 Withholding time

It is rare that sufficient numbers of cows will retain antibiotics longer than the withholding time given by the manufacturers on the treatment to cause a milk tank failure. Since the antibiotic in the udder is 'flushed out' by milk, low yields, brought about by milk fever, etc., may extend retention times and in such cases it may be sensible to extend withholding times or seek advice.

10.3.4 Dry cow therapy

Such treatments tend to be long acting (in an oil base), hence early calving dry cows may excrete antibiotics for some time after calving making it essential that drying off dates are recorded.

10.3.5 Other treatments

If it has been necessary to treat a cow not only with an intramammary infusion but also by intramuscular injection it will be necessary to seek and action veterinary advice about retention times since they may be extended.

10.3.6 Milking plant contamination

Farmers who carefully follow withholding times can still have a bulk vat failure if they allow milk high in antibiotic residues to contaminate the milking line surfaces other than at the end of milking. It should be borne in mind that the test is sensitive to 0.006 international units of penicillin per ml of milk (IU/ml), yet a cow may have been infused with a million or more IU. Even if the cluster and milking jar are washed after keeping the contaminated milk out of the bulk vat, faulty valves or poor plant design may let contaminated milk into the vat. The only safe course is to milk treated cows last when the rest of the herd has been milked or preferably to use a separate bucket and cluster.

10.4 Hormones (BST)

Cow's milk, being a natural body fluid, contains glandular and tissue hormones which are species specific to the cow. The cow's milk production is stimulated by a message carried by the hormone somatotropin from the pituitary gland of the brain. Bovine somatotropin (BST) is a protein containing 190–191 amino acids.

In recent years *Escherichia coli* have been genetically engineered to produce recombined BST (rBST), which is almost identical to natural BST. Genetically produced BST was developed as it took the extract of about 20 cow brains to produce sufficient BST for a small daily dose for one cow.

The difference between BST and rBST is small. rBST is up to 194 amino acids in length and lacks a methionine amino acid substitution at the chain end. The human somatotropin is very different from the bovine hormone and this explains why BST is quite ineffective in man. Hormones can best be described as a key and the configuration of the BST 'key' is very different from that of human somatotropin making it fit the bovine but not the human 'lock'. BST has in the past been injected into human pituitary dwarfs with no effect at all.

When rBST is given to the lactating cow, usually as an intramuscular or subcutaneous injection, it increases her own natural BST levels and stimulates increased milk production. Milk production is boosted by the increased BST levels and the appetite for food intake increases with the efficiency of feed conversion being increased.

The strategic uses of BST applications include producing the same amount of milk from fewer cows, increasing milk production at time of low-cost home-grown feed and using BST to accelerate production to meet quota. It is claimed that BST use will increase milk production by 4–7 litres/day.

Whilst treatment may increase levels of BST in milk it is not possible—even with the most sophisticated radioimmunoassay techniques—to differentiate between natural and rBST, nor are levels very different from the natural range found in milk. BST and rBST are inactivated by normal pasteurisation. When BST is ingested in raw milk it is broken down into its amino acids in the gut, as with any protein. BST and rBST are not considered to be of any health risk to man.

The composition of milk from BST-treated cows is not significantly different from normal milk—although there is a tendency for somatic cell counts to increase.

rBST usage is a question being wrestled with in the Western world. Although rBST is licensed for use in some countries, questions about the 'unnatural' nature of 'BST-produced milk', social economic effects on farming and questions about animal health and welfare have resulted in its widespread use being delayed.

10.5 Disinfectants

In order to sterilise dairy plants and limit the spread of mastitis organisms, disinfectants are used on milking plants and for teat disinfection. Care has to be taken to limit residues which find access to milk.

Iodine is the most effective antimicrobial agent and is used as the iodine–potassium iodide complex 'iodophor', usually in the presence of a wetting agent. This mixture is extremely efficient and kills all mastitic germs within a few seconds. Alternatives to iodine are chlorhexidine (hibitane) and hypochlorite.

Iodine is an essential element for man, however adverse reactions (thyrotoxicosis) have been associated with excess intake. For this reason the content of iodine in the teat dipping formulation should be limited to a maximum of 0.3% available iodine, which will guarantee that the additional iodine content of milk will not exceed 150 µg/kg.

The iodine content of milk with and without teat disinfection shows that providing teat dipping is undertaken sensibly it does not give rise to high levels in milk. The iodine used in mineral supplement feeds has a greater influence on levels in milk.

The daily intake of iodine by man is recommended to be 150–300 µg/day and a target upper value maximum for milk is 500µg/kg.

10.6   Nitrates, nitrites and nitrosamines

Nitrates and nitrites are associated with the formation of carcinogenic nitrosamines in the gut. However, the incidence of nitrates, nitrites and nitrosamines is not a problem with milk as it comes from the cow. Nitrates are used to control the bacteriological problem of late blowing in cheese and nitric acid has been used to descale milking and dairy plants. These are the major potential sources of nitrates in dairy products which require strict control.

10.7   Pesticides

10.7.1   Incidence

At one time the environmentally persistent organochlorine (OC) pesticides were widely used; DDT as insecticide, endrin as rodenticide and HCB as a fungicide on crops. The replacement of these by the less stable, hence less environmentally persistent organophosphorous (OP) pesticides, has reduced the levels of OC residues found in the environment and in milk.

The supervised use of pesticides is however still necessary in agriculture in order to minimise crop losses. OC residues may therefore still find access to milk from earlier contamination of the environment, from application of sewage sludge being applied to land or from cattle feedstuffs imported from developing countries where OC pesticides are still used.

Table 10.3 ADI values for chlorinated hydrocarbon pesticides[a]

Compound	ADI (mg/kg body weight)	Compound	ADI (mg/kg body weight)
Aldrin and Dieldrin	0.0001	Endosulphane	0.006
Chlorbenside	0.01	Heptochlor and epoxides	0.0005
Chlordane	0.0005	Lindane (γ- BHC)	0.008
Chlorbenzilate	0.02	α- BHC	0.005
Chlopropylate	0.01	β- BHC	0.001
DDT (and metabolites)	0.02	Methoxychlor	0.1

[a]Source: World Health Organization.

OC pesticides are fat soluble. Man is at the end of the food chain hence accumulates any ingested OC pesticides in his body fat. Lactating women mobilise body fat to produce a rather restricted milk fat yield (20–25 g/day) for a short period of time, hence about 8% or more of their accumulated levels of OC residues are excreted in breast-milk fat during one breast-feeding period. It is also a fact that human breast milk, unlike cow's milk, is not mixed with other milks before being consumed. These factors lead to individual samples of human milk being significantly higher in OC residues than cow's milk.

10.7.2 Significance of residues

The World Health Organization (FAO/WHO) have set ADI levels which are used as residue maxima to ensure consumer safety (Table 10.3). It can be demonstrated (assuming the average adult consumes 40 g of butterfat per day), based on analyses of OC residues in milk in a number of European countries, that the levels found in milk pose no threat to health.

OP, carbamate and pyrethroid insecticides are not normally found in milk.

10.7.3 Limiting residues in milk

The levels of residues in milk fat should be checked against MRLs. Generally, levels now being recorded are low compared with ADI levels and are declining. Good agricultural practice should minimise the OC residues in dairy cattle feed and levels should be frequently monitored in imported feeds.

Test methods involve extraction of the fat from milk followed by separation and identification of OC residues using gas chromatography.

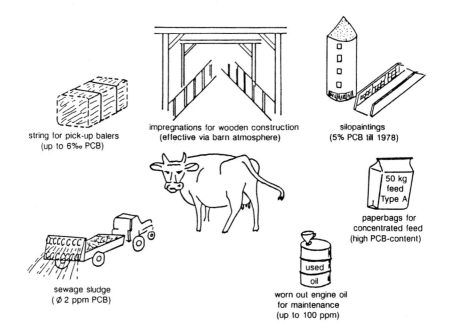

Figure 10.2   Potential sources of PCBs in milk.

10.8   PCBs

Polychlorinated biphenyls (PCBs) are found in the environment as a result of their industrial use. PCBs are a mixture of over 200 differently chlorinated biphenyls used in hydraulic systems, insulators, plasticisers, heat exchangers, printing, etc.

It is estimated that over one million tonnes of PCBs has been produced since 1929. PCBs are extremely stable, hence these highly toxic materials have found their way into the environment and the food chain. Like OC pesticides, PCBs are fat soluble and are secreted in the milk fat of the lactating cow after transfer from the body fat of the cow. Figure 10.2 shows potential sources of contamination.

Whilst normal background levels in milk are acceptably low and well within official threshhold levels (50 µg/kg fat) levels may rise if the cow is subjected to high-risk exposure. For this reason it is sensible for milk to be surveyed for PCBs from time to time.

10.9 Mycotoxins

Mycotoxins are the toxic biproducts of moulds. The major mycotoxin of importance to milk is aflatoxin M_1 (AFM_1) which derives from aflatoxin B (AFB) found on forage. These aflatoxins are believed to be carcinogens hence need to be controlled in milk—especially that used for infant feed.

AFB_1 occurs in forage contaminated with the mould *Aspergillus flavus* which grows under warm moist conditions. AFB_1 is therefore more likely to be found in concentrates such as ground nut cake, copra, etc. imported from Third World tropical countries.

AFB_1 fed to a dairy cow, is hydroxylated to the metabolite AFM_1—the only mycotoxin of significance in milk. About one-fiftieth of the ingested AFB_1 carries over to milk as the M_1 metabolite. From this data, established from feeding trials, it is possible to calculate the upper limit which should be set for feedingstuffs in order to control AFM_1 levels in milk.

The EU legal tolerance for AFB_1 in ruminant feed is 5 µg/kg dry matter. As stated earlier, groundnut cake, copra, cotton and palm cake show occasional high contamination by AFB_1.

There is a need for careful control therefore by compounders to ensure that legal limits are not exceeded and that suppliers to them of raw materials use harvesting and storage conditions which will limit AFB_1 growth.

Surveys of AFM_1 in milk in the late 1970s in Europe showed many samples were positive, albeit at a low level. A recent survey has shown levels in milk to be sporadic and low (<10 ng/kg) however careful control over AFB_1 levels in concentrates being compounded for dairy cattle feed is necessary to keep levels of AFM in milk to an absolute minimum.

10.10 Toxic metals

Cadmium, lead and mercury are the toxic trace metals of significance to man and are a 'threat' to our foodstuffs by virtue of industrial usage (Figure 10.3).

10.10.1 Lead

Milk and milk products play an important part in man's diet and contribute greatly to the diet of the young, therefore concern about the global pollution of the environment has led to many studies of the pathways of heavy metals into milk.

Lead is a threat to man via his/her food and drink or inhalation. Chronic lead poisoning is caused by long exposure at levels of about 1 mg/day. Man has contributed significantly to the environmental pollution

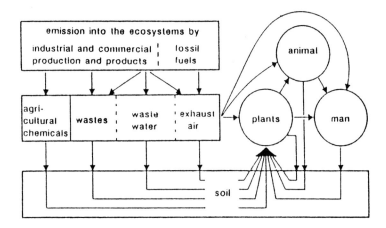

Figure 10.3 Pathways of heavy metals in the industrial world.

with lead which he has used in batteries, paints, alloys and as an anti-knock in petrol. Milk itself does not come into contact with lead, except possibly in canned milks where soldered joints historically caused problems. This was overcome by lacquering the interior of cans.

Contamination is possible through ingestion by the cow, since her feedstuffs may be contaminated. Studies on milk produced in clear mountain areas and near to motorways however have shown that milk from both areas have acceptably low levels of lead. Feeding of fodder 'spiked' with lead has demonstrated that much of the lead fed to dairy cattle does not enter the milk. The cow acts as a very effective biological filter diverting lead from her feed to her bones rather than to her milk.

This first line of defence by the cow was very useful in practice in the early 1990s when rice bran imported into the UK was heavily contaminated with a lead salt. Whilst the contaminated feedstuff increased levels of lead in milk, at no time were levels a serious risk to human health.

Tolerable weekly intakes based on chronic toxicological studies have been set for lead. Even when allowing for a high consumption of milk (1.5 litres/week), the weekly intake of lead through milk consumption would be less than 2% of the tolerable weekly intake since the levels of lead found in milk (0.002 mg/kg) are extremely low.

10.10.2   Cadmium

Cadmium, like lead, is a cumulative poison hence levels in food should be kept to a minimum. A significant part of man's intake results from inhalation from air contaminated by cadmium, and cigarette smokers increase their intake by 25–50%.

In Japan prolonged ingestion of rice contaminated with cadmium from a nearby mine produced 'itai–itai—disease' and demonstrated the dangers of environmental contamination. As with lead the only threat to milk comes from forage and fertilisation of feedstuffs with sewage sludge. Again, as with lead, the cow acts as an effective biological filter and the proportion of ingested cadmium finding access to milk is extremely small. Milk and milk products therefore contribute a negligible amount to the weekly acceptable intakes set by FAO/WHO.

10.10.3 Mercury

Cow's milk very seldom exceeds 0.002 mg/kg due to the effective filtering mechanism of the cow. Compared with the acceptable daily intake of 0.04 mg mercury it can be concluded that milk and milk products are safe and make little contribution to the mercury intake of man. An average daily consumption of 1 litre of milk or milk products delivers less than 1.5% of the tolerable weekly intake.

10.11 Dioxins

Dioxins are a group of highly toxic chemicals produced by a range of processes from chlorination of wood pulp used in cartoning material to burning organic material in the presence of chlorine. Dioxins are often referred to as PCDDs and PCDFs—polychlorinated dibenzodioxins and polychlorinated dibenzofurans.

Dioxins, being persistent chemicals, are widely spread in the environment. Their presence in foodstuffs is very low and analysis for dioxins is very expensive since analytical techniques capable of measuring accurately to 10 parts in a quadrillion (one thousand million million) are required to detect them. Levels are monitored in foodstuffs and since dairy products can contribute about a quarter of the dietary intake of dioxins, milk forms part of food monitoring programmes.

Levels of dioxins in milk can only be reduced at source by control of industrial incinerators. Surveys show that dioxin levels from farms in rural areas are lower than those from industrial areas especially those near to industrial incinerators. Emission of dioxin from incinerators can be reduced however by control of incineration temperatures.

'Hot spot' areas for the very stable dioxins have been found. In the UK, for example, in Derbyshire in the early 1990s, heavy contamination was found on some farms and in the milk from those farms following heavy deposition of dioxins, believed to be possibly associated with a major industrial fire and explosion some 25 years earlier.

There is little farmers can do to control dioxin levels in milk as they have to rely on environmental studies which point to and direct industrialists to control emissions.

As with most of the contaminants detailed in this chapter regular surveillance of foodstuffs is required to check that milk meets regulatory standards. Surveys generally show that milk has an extremely good track record in terms of safety, as the industry has shown a good response to minimising the level of undesirable contaminants in milk.

10.12   Radionuclides in milk

On the 26 April 1986 an accident occurred at Chernobyl near Kiev in the Ukraine, causing substantial quantities of radioactive material to be released into the atmosphere. This incident focused attention on the dangers of radionuclides in the food chain.

The cloud of airborne radioactive material emitted from Chernobyl was deposited in the rain and found access to the food chain through vegetables, meat and dairy products.

10.12.1   What is radioactivity?

Certain chemical elements are formed in unstable states which spontaneously decay as they change to more stable forms. During this change they emit radioactivity as α particles, β particles or γ-rays (Table 10.4). Such radioactive atoms are called radionuclides. The emissions from radionuclides can bring about changes in substances which are in their path.

In living tissues they can lead to development of cancers or genetic abnormalities. The penetrating power of the emissions differ.

10.12.2   Radioactive decay

Whilst all radionuclides are unstable, the times taken for different nuclides to decay varies and this is called 'the half-life'. The half-life is the time taken for one half of the nuclides in a sample to decay or in other words, the time for a radioisotope to lose half of its activity. The rate of decay or half-life is specific for each isotope and can vary from a few seconds to millions of years. For example iodine-131 has a half-life of 8 days, which means that after 8 days only half of the activity will remain; after 16 days 25% is left; after 24 days 12.5% is left and so on. After seven half-lives there will be less than 1% of the original level of activity. For iodine-131 therefore it would take 7 times 8 days, i.e. 56 days for the level of radia-

Table 10.4 Radioactive emission and penetrating power

Emission	Nature	Shield needed to absorb emission
α particles	Two protons and two neutrons (positively charged)	Two sheets of paper or thin aluminium foil
β particles	Electrons (negatively charged)	2 mm aluminium
γ ray	Electromagnetic radiation (no charge)	50 cm concrete or 10 cm lead
Neutrons	Subatomic particles (no charge)	Several metres of concrete

tion to reduce to 1% of its original level. Iodine-131 has a short half-life but other radionuclides can have very long half-lives. Caesium-137, for example, has a half-life of 30 years and it would take 210 years for the radioactivity to reduce to 1% of the original. Carbon-14, a slow decay radionuclide, has an even longer half-life of 5730 years and uranium-238 a half-life of 4 500 000 000 years.

10.12.3 Our exposure to radiation

Some radiation reaches us from outer space as cosmic rays. We are also exposed to radiation from naturally radioactive elements on earth. Rocks and particularly granite emit radiation. It is estimated that only 10% of normal exposure comes from man-made radioactivity: medical X-rays, luminous paints, atomic tests, nuclear reactors, etc. Whilst man has added to this earth's level of radioactivity through nuclear weapons, nuclear fuel plants such as Chernobyl, and even luminous watch dials, it is estimated that about 95% of man's exposure from man-made sources, is from this use of radiation in medicine, i.e. X-rays. About 5% is estimated to come from fallout and less than 1% from nuclear power generation.

10.12.4 How do we measure radiation levels?

10.12.4.1 Units. Becquerels are used as a measure of activity or the rate at which spontaneous decay occurs. The becquerel is defined as 'one disintegration per second'. The curie (the old unit of activity) is 2.7×10^{11} becquerels.

The dose equivalent is the sievert which enables a comparison of the potential biological harm from different types of ionising radiation. The sievert modifies the dose absorbed to produce an estimate of the biological harm.

The absorbed dose measured in grays is the amount of energy from ionising radiation absorbed by a medium. This absorption varies with the type of material (air, water or body tissue) but one gray corresponds to the absorption of one joule per kg of the medium.

As stated earlier this absorbed dose is not necessarily the dose equivalent. For β particles γ- and X-rays they are, and one gray equals 1 sievert. α particles, however, have a much greater biological effect than β particles hence for α particles one gray corresponds to a 20 sievert dose equivalent.

10.12.4.2 Practical measurement. Measurement of radioactivity is highly specialised. Scintillation counters are used to measure surface radioactivity; they measure the disintegration rate of the radionuclide. To measure the amount of radioactive material in a sample, α, β and γ emitters need to be used separately.

10.12.5   Access to milk

Radionuclides are deposited by rain hence find their way into the human and animal food supply. In some crops (mushrooms and reindeer moss) radionuclides are concentrated whereas for grass, contamination is simply by deposition. When cows graze they eat the grass and any radionuclides deposited on it. Since milk is easy to mix and sample, milk is often used as an indicator of deposition of radionuclides. Milk is also the primary source of food for babies which makes it necessary to check milk on a regular basis.

Disasters such as Chernobyl create a major human problem but do offer scientists an opportunity to gather information on the impact of radionuclides on the food chain. Clearly, the amount of deposition across Europe varied according to the movement of the cloud of radionuclides and the rainfall causing deposition.

Studies in areas of lightest contamination showed that contamination of meat and milk from sheep was greater than from cows. It is believed that this is due to the fact that sheep ingest more soil when grazing, and soil will have a higher deposition of nuclides than grass.

The Chernobyl cloud contained, amongst other nuclides, iodine-131. Although this is a short half-life radionuclide it represents a threat since iodine is concentrated in the thyroid gland whereas other nuclides, such as caesium tend to be distributed around the body. For this reason milk in excess of 500 Bq/litre was made into long shelf-life products such as cheese or milk powder and only milk below this figure was used for short shelf-life products, following the Chernobyl disaster. A grazing ban was introduced which meant that cows were taken indoors and fed conserved foods harvested before the Chernobyl accident. Such simple measures helped to retain consumer confidence whilst levels of radioactivity, due to short half-life radionuclides fell quickly.

10.12.6   The risk in perspective

There is no doubt that consumers are concerned about contaminants such as radionuclides in milk. Normal levels of radioactivity in milk however are below 5 Bq/litre, somewhat below 1/600th of the level causing concern about human health. Levels found in the UK during the peak of deposition from Chernobyl were also low compared with normal background levels.

The International Commission on Radiological Protection considers that the maximum allowable dose, over and above that derived from natural and medical sources, is an additional 5 mSv. The calculated additional dose received by a UK adult as a result of Chernobyl in 1987 was 0.3 mSv in areas of high deposition and 0.02 in areas of low deposition.

10.12.7   Partition of radionuclides in dairy products

Commercial dairy products have been made from milk known to be contaminated with radionuclides. Radio-caesium was shown to partition in the aqueous phase leaving butter, cream and cheese with lower levels than skim. Ion exchange demineralisation was found to be effective in removing radio-caesium from whey. Berlin blue (ammonium hexa-cyanoferrate) and bentonite have both been used to remove radioactive caesium from milk.

The subject of radionuclides is sometimes confused in consumers' minds with that of food irradiation.

10.13   Irradiation

When liquid milk is irradiated, OH radicals are formed from water, which accelerates the oxidation of milk fat and produces off-flavours. The dose needed to sterilise raw milk by ionising-irradiation is higher than 15 kGy and although lower doses can be used with a supplementary heat treatment, off-flavours have been reported at as low as 0.2–0.5 kGy. The shelf-life of pasteurised milk irradiated (at 0.25 kGy) at room temperature and stored at 4°C increased by a factor of 2 compared to non-irradiated milk with no flavour impairment.

It has been suggested that irradiation followed by heat treatment would be more effective since bacteria are more sensitive to heat after being irradiated. The irradiation of dairy products has however not found favour due partially to the flavour impairment of fat oxidation and partially to the negative image which food irradiation still carries in the mind of the consumer.

Further reading

Contaminants

Egmond, H.P., van (1989) *Mycotoxins in Dairy Products.* Elsevier Applied Science, London, UK, p. 282.
IDF (1987) *Milk and Milk Products: Detection of Inhibitors* (Bulletin 220). IDF, Brussels, Belgium.
IDF (1991) *Monograph on Residues and Contaminants in Milk and Dairy Products.* (Special Issue 9101). IDF, Brussels, Belgium.

Radionuclides in milk

Assimakopoulos, P.A *et al.* (1987) Transport of the radioisotopes iodine-131, caesium-134 and caesium -137 from the fall out following the accident at the Chernobyl nuclear reactor into cheese and other cheesemaking products. *J. Dairy Sci.,* **70**, 1338–1343.
Fry, F.A *et al.* (1986) Early estimates of UK radiation doses from the Chernobyl reactor. *Nature,* **321**, 193–195.
Lagoni, H. *et al.* (1963) Studies on the quantitative distribution of radioactive fallout products in milk. *Milchwissenschaft,* **18**, 340–344.
National Radiological Protection Board (1981) *Living with radiation.* HMSO, London, UK.
Wilson, L. *et al.* (1988) Transfer of radioactive contamination from milk to commercial dairy products. *J. Soc. Diary Technol.,* **41**(1).

11 Nutritional aspects

F. HARDING

11.1 Introduction

Milk is the natural food of the young and has been described as close to being nature's perfect food. It has a wide range of positive nutritional benefits and supplies a variety of nutrients including protein for body building, vitamins, minerals (especially calcium) and fat and carbohydrate for energy. The contribution milk makes to individual diets will vary from country to country but using the UK diet as an example, in 1990 milk and milk products supplied a quarter of the protein, between one-half and two-thirds of the calcium, over one-quarter of the riboflavin (vitamin B_2) and about a half of the vitamin A of the average diet.

The early study of nutrition in many countries tended to focus on the effect of food deficiencies on health. In affluent countries, however, attention has recently focused on the effect of dietary excesses on health. Milk and milk products (excluding butter) provide about one-sixth of the UK dietary fat and a quarter of the intake of saturated fat, making milk, in spite of its nutritional attributes, a target for attack.

Concern about the impact of diet on health is not new. In AD 600 Romans were accused of 'digging their own graves —with their teeth'. Sadly, whilst some people in developing countries are starving, many people in the West have more than enough to eat and concern has grown about the role of excess dietary fat in coronary heart disease and cancer; the role of salt in the development of hypertension and strokes; of sugar in dental caries; of an excess of calories in obesity; and of a number of specific foods in provoking allergies and intolerance.

In the 1930s and 1940s the science of nutrition was concerned with identification of the important nutrients in the diet, such as the vitamins. Boyd-Orr in the UK, McCallum in the USA and Den Hartog in Continental Europe considered the positive value of nutrients to the solution of many of the world's problems and recognised the contribution made by milk. The image of milk, at its peak in the 1930s, was tarnished in the 1970s and 1980s when the role of diet in degenerative diseases such as cancer and heart disease were debated. The debate on the role of fat in the diet was raised with the laudable objective of reducing the incidence of coronary disease. However, scientific findings have often been misinterpreted in a desire to find a quick and simple solution.

Whilst many nutritionists extol the virtue of a balanced diet some have failed to recognise the need for balance in food advice and propaganda—leaving the consumer somewhat confused about the safety and nutritional value of foodstuffs.

Most nutritionists agree however that there is no such thing as a bad food—only good or bad diets—and milk and dairy products have a significant role to play as part of a balanced diet.

11.2   Milk fat

Fats are components of the brain, nerve cells and are essential to many physiological processes. Milk fat, being an animal fat, is characterised as being a 'saturated fat' however about 32% of milk's fatty acids are unsaturated—primarily oleic acid ($C_{18:1}$). Most of milk's unsaturated fatty acids are monounsaturates and current research has shown that cattle feeding practices could raise the monounsaturates level of milk to well over 40%. Epidemiological studies indicate that Mediterranean countries have low levels of heart disease. It has been suggested that this, in part, is because of their high levels of dietary monounsaturated fatty acids.

Milk supplies the essential fatty acids linoleic acid (2.1%), lanoleic acid (0.5%) and arachidonic acid (0.14%). These are required by the body for normal metabolism and growth. Short (C_2 to C_6) and medium chain (C_8 to C_{12}) fatty acids account for about 12% of the fatty acids of milk and being more readily digested do not contribute to the elevation of blood lipids nor are they deposited in adipose tissue.

Fats are calorie dense providing about 9.4 kcal/g. Fats are stored by the body as a source of energy and those watching their weight are advised to reduce fat intake as part of their calorie reduction. This can be achieved without cutting milk or dairy products out of the diet since the dairy industry produces a wide range of different products to meet different dietary needs.

Milk may be consumed unaltered 'as it comes from the cow' (about 4% fat). The fat content may be increased—some countries market high-fat (about 8%) breakfast milks. Many countries produce 'standardised' milk at 3.5% fat or 'semi-skimmed' ('half fat') milk at 1.6% fat or skim-milk which is virtually fat-free at less than 0.3% fat. The flavour and 'mouth feel' of the higher fat milks have an indulgence appeal whereas skim-milk is an acquired taste by those following a dietary regime.

There is therefore no need to curb milk intake in order to reduce fat intake, one can choose to drink low-fat milks. Whilst skim-milks are deficient in fat-soluble vitamins such as A, D, E and K, they are still a good source of water-soluble vitamins, minerals and protein. Some countries allow the fortification of standardised milk with added fat-soluble vitamins, provided the milk is adequately labelled. It should also be remembered that fat makes high-fibre foods such as cereals and bread palatable as well as slowing the digestive system.

11.3 Dietary cholesterol

Cholesterol is a natural substance found in body tissues. The human body contains over 100 g of cholesterol which is an essential component of all membranes, the starting point for the manufacture of bile salts for digestion, for steroid hormones and for vitamin D. About 75% of our daily needs are made in the body and the remainder is obtained from the diet. Metabolic control of the body's synthesis of cholesterol ensures production rises or falls to compensate for our dietary intake. However, some people have an inherited defect—familial hypercholesterolaemia—which affects this control and can lead to excessively high blood levels of cholesterol. Hence, the amount of cholesterol concentration in blood is affected by hereditary and partly by environmental factors such as intake of saturated fatty acids, exercising or alcohol consumption. Except for those people who have a very high blood level of cholesterol, cholesterol in the diet has virtually no impact on the concentration in blood.

Whilst cholesterol in the body is of importance, the impact of cholesterol in the diet has largely been quite unjustifiably overemphasised.

11.4 Proteins

Proteins are the body's 'building blocks' affecting our growth and immunity. Antibodies, enzymes and hormones all contain proteins. Thus the proteins we eat provide the amino acids needed to replace both these and essential body cells. Whilst the body is able to synthesise some amino acids there are eight which it cannot make and these are the essential amino acids. Histidine is also considered to be essential for infants. The essential amino acids have to be supplied in our food proteins and all, unlike many other foods, are found in milk.

The acid conditions in the stomach untangle proteins laying them open to attack by enzymes called proteases. The broken fragments are then used to provide the body's amino acid requirements. Proteins in excess of the body's requirements are used for energy.

Milk provides easily digested protein of a high nutritional value and is a rich source of essential amino acids (Table 11.1).

11.5 Milk allergy and intolerance

Consumption of certain foods can produce unpleasant effects and whilst this phenomenon has been recognised for a long time it has been given wider publicity in recent years.

Table 11.1   Essential amino acids

Amino acid	Daily requirement (g)	g/100g Milk protein
Phenylalanine	1.1	5.5
Methionine	1.1	2.8
Leucine	1.1	12.1
Valine	0.8	7.1
Lysine	0.8	7.4
Isoleucine	0.7	6.7
Threonine	0.5	4.6
Tryptophan	0.3	1.4
Histidine[a]	80	2.2

[a]mg/kg.

The two conditions are often confused. However, there is a difference between food intolerance and food allergy. Generally, food intolerance is a term used to cover any adverse reaction to foods and involves, for example, a lack of the enzyme necessary to digest a specific food; for example, lactose intolerance; a second example is the presence of a toxin in foods which irritates the lining of the intestine. A true food allergy, however, will be due to a reaction involving the body's immune system and is usually in response to a protein.

Adverse food reactions may be blamed for abdominal pain, vomiting, diarrhoea or skin symptoms such as urticaria and eczema, respiratory problems, hyperactivity, arthritis and even migraine. The extent to which food is guilty is not fully understood as many other aspects of the environment can illicit similar reactions.

11.5.1   Lactose intolerance

There is a need for the enzyme lactase to be present in the small intestine to break the disaccharide lactose into the simpler smaller molecular sugars glucose and galactose prior to its absorption (see Figure 6.9). If lactase is not present, lactose passes into the large intestine where it provides an active medium for intestinal bacteria such as coliforms; this can lead to abdominal pain and flatulence.

Normally babies are born with lactase but in later life when their dependence on milk reduces levels of the enzyme fall. Lactose intolerance therefore tends to affect adults rather than young children.

Milk has been traditionally included in the diets of white northern Europeans and adequate levels of the enzyme persist into adulthood. However, lactase deficiency is widespread in South East Asia, India, the Middle East and Africa where milk drinking after infancy is uncommon. It is estimated that 70% of such populations show lactose intolerance whereas for people of northern European stock the figure is less than 6%. UHT milk supplied in areas where lactase deficiency is a problem may be 'spiked' with the enzyme in order to break down lactose during storage. This also makes the milk taste much sweeter due to the glucose produced.

If lactose intolerance is suspected it is sensible to seek advice from a dietician, who may advise the removal of milk and milk products containing lactose from the diet to see if the symptoms vanish and reoccur when milk is reintroduced. Such indirect methods may not be conclusive, however, and direct measurement techniques involving measurement of blood sugar after consumption of a standard amount of lactose, measurement of breath hydrogen after oral consumption of lactose and testing stools for acidity are more reliable.

The solution to the problem may be simple. Most people who suffer from lactose intolerance only suffer if they have a large dose of lactose at one time. Most people can drink a glass of milk (250 ml) without discomfort or they can purchase milk in which lactose has been hydrolysed. Fat-containing milk is better tolerated than skim-milk. Many cultured products such as yogurts have had much of the lactose hydrolysed by bacterial lactase and products such as cheese have virtually no lactose once it is lost to the whey in the cheesemaking process.

11.5.2 Milk allergy

A very different complaint is milk protein allergy or milk protein hypersensitivity. The incidence is believed to be very small, and tends to affect babies; about 1 case per 5000 births. The problem is not unique to cow's milk but is associated with the introduction of foreign proteins early in life. It is seen in particular among children with a family history of allergy, and its appearance often follows a bout of gastroenteritis. Most children have outgrown the reaction by the time they go to school.

The symptoms may include vomiting, diarrhoea or skin disorders such as eczema. As with lactose intolerance, trial and error may help pinpoint the problem, by removing from the diet under controlled conditions, one at a time, cow's milk and cow's milk products and other foods such as egg—to see if symptoms improve. Exclusion diets of this nature must always be used under medical supervision to avoid undermining the child's nutritional status or growth. This is because elimination of milk products from the diet may cause calcium deficiency or contribute to other forms of malnutrition. Using double-blind food challenges to reintroduce the suspected food helps to avoid misinterpretation of the cause of the allergy.

With babies and young children, if avoidance of cow's milk products is found to be necessary, it is essential that they are replaced by a suitable alternative milk formula. A specialised formula based on milk protein hydrolysates may be the answer as these are unlikely to cause allergy. Soya-based formulae are sometimes recommended but soya protein can also provoke an allergic reaction in a significant number of infants who react to cow's milk protein. Heat treatment of milk protein may reduce the allergenicity. Boiled or UHT milk may be tolerated, even though fresh milk may not, among older children.

It has been suggested that the use of goat's milk may avoid the risk of allergy, but goat's milk protein is as likely as cow's milk protein to provide an allergic reaction.

11.6   Cultured or fermented milks

It is believed that fermented milks may have originated in the Middle East as early as 1300 BC as a means of preserving milk. They then spread through Central and Eastern Europe. The common link is that they are all based on lactic fermentation either by a single or a mixture of organisms.

There is a considerable mystique about cultured milks and milk products. Their health benefits have been extolled for years with tales of longevity in Eastern Europe being attributed to yogurts containing *Streptococcus bulgaricus*. Although solid scientific backing for health claims is limited, cultured milk and dairy products are growing in popularity as health foods.

The composition of milk is subtly changed by microorganisms used in cultured milks. Proteins are partially degraded to peptides and amino acids, fats are hydrolysed—releasing fatty acids—and lactose is converted to glucose and galactose which in turn are changed to produce a variety of organic acids which yield the 'sharp' flavours of cultured products. Cultured milks therefore have a changed composition, as well as an accumulation of the products of bacterial fermentations and antimicrobial compounds emitted by the culture organisms in order to inhibit the growth of other organisms.

Any health-promoting properties of cultured products may therefore be due to the changed composition of milk, the bacterial metabolites released by the culture or from beneficial effects of the live bacteria on the immune system of the consumer of the yogurt.

Two cultures, *Lactobacillus acidophilus* and *Bifidobacterium bifidis*, are being more widely used in cultured products. *Lactobacillus acidophilus* is used in the USA to produce 'sweet acidophilus milks'. These are made by adding a frozen concentrate of a human isolate of *L. acidophilus* to a cold, pasteurised low-fat milk which is maintained at below 4°C. About seven million *L. acidophilus* organisms per ml milk can be present and the product keeps for 2–3 weeks in the refrigerator.

Japanese claims that bifidobacteria rather than *L. acidophilus* predominate in the human gastrointestinal tract have led to a greater interest in bifidus products in Japan.

It is believed that live yogurts (as opposed to 'dead' yogurts where cultured products, pasteurised *after* culturing thus killing the culture organisms in order to lengthen the shelf-life) may have health-giving properties by

(a) protecting against human intestinal infections by acting as probiotics in the human gut;

(b) improving the digestion and utilisation of lactose since lactose is better tolerated by lactase-deficient individuals when it is taken in the form of cultured products;

(c) reducing blood cholesterol: certain gut microflora can metabolise cholesterol hence cultured milks may lower man's plasma cholesterol;

(d) protection against cancer: it has been suggested that some lactobacilli produce anti-carcinogenic compounds and bacteria may metabolise and destroy known carcinogens such as nitrosamines.

11.7   Immune milk

Bacteria and viruses, referred to as antigens, are recognised by the body's immune system as foreign and undesirable. The body as part of its natural defence produces antibodies, large protein molecules which bind to and hence control these antigens.

It has been long recognised that a mother's milk provides an array of immune factors to help protect her young against infections. Regular immunisation with a proprietory vaccine containing sterilised dead specific bacteria is now adopted commercially in New Zealand in order to induce cows to produce antibodies to specific bacteria. The antibodies are then secreted by the cow into her milk which is processed for human consumption. Consumption of this milk produces an immunity in the consumer similar to that which a nursing mother provides for her newborn child.

The antibodies in immune milk are resistant to digestive enzymes and reach the lower gut of the person consuming milk where they control the growth and proliferation of harmful gut bacteria.

11.8   Minerals

11.8.1   Calcium

Calcium, phosphorus, sodium and potassium account for about 4% by weight of the fat-free human body. Calcium therefore is a dietary essential.

In many Western countries milk and dairy products contribute between 50 and 60% of average calcium intake, and in a form which is readily utilised. Vitamin D is essential in calcium absorption which is also enhanced in the presence of lactose. Not all calcium eaten is absorbed (typically about 30%) and the presence of phytates, for example, from high-fibre diets—further reduce calcium availability by locking it into a complex thereby preventing absorption and subsequent utilisation. Not only is milk a readily usable source of calcium, it is believed that it may also enhance the bioavailability of calcium from other food sources.

Osteoporosis is a disorder of the skeleton which occurs during ageing and increases the risk of bone fractures. Osteoporosis is particularly prevalent amongst post-menopausal women although it may also occur in older men.

Nutritionists now believe that there is value in having a regular intake of calcium throughout one's lifetime in order to develop and maintain optimum bone health and that this creation of peak bone mass helps reduce the risk of osteoporosis occurring later in life. Physical exercise is also important for all age groups.

Bone mass peaks in the 20–30 year age group after which it declines. Therefore it is of particular importance that teenage girls and young women in an attempt to remain slim do not forego milk and milk products as part of their diets. Low-fat milks, equally rich in calcium but lower in calories, are a valuable part of a slimming diet.

11.8.2 Trace elements

The importance of trace elements in human nutrition is becoming more clearly understood and recent developments in trace analysis have meant that very low levels, from 1 part per billion to a few parts per million, can now be measured with greater accuracy.

Trace elements tend to be classified as 'essential', 'non-essential' and 'toxic'. There are 26 naturally occurring elements essential to animal life of which 15 are accepted as being trace elements and many of these occur in milk. Certain elements such as arsenic are essential at low levels but become toxic if consumed at high levels. Therefore, in many countries a minimum requirement for essential elements and a 'safe' dietary maximum level for the potentially dangerous toxic elements have been set and are discussed elsewhere in this book.

Trace elements in cow's milk largely originate from the feed. Milk, a naturally designed food for the young calf, is a good source of a broad-based cocktail of trace elements in forms, unlike some mineral tablet supplements that can be readily assimilated by the body. This is why milk is referred to as an almost complete food.

Cow's milk contains traces of aluminium, arsenic, barium, boron, bromine, cadmium, chromium, cobalt, copper, fluorine, iodine, iron, lead, manganese, molybdenum, nickel, sodium, selenium, silicon, silver, tin, vanadium and zinc.

11.8.2.1 Zinc.   Zinc is an essential constituent of over 40 of the body's enzymes and plays an important role in maintaining the appetite and in the promotion of wound healing. Dietary zinc defficiency can therefore lead to extensive skin lesions, a decline in the resistance to infection, depression, lethargy and a decline in appetite. Zinc deficiency has been associated with anorexia nervosa. Adequate dietary zinc is particularly important during periods of rapid growth and development and especially during recovery from infection or physical injury.

Milk is a relatively important source of zinc, contributing for average milk drinkers about a quarter of the recommended daily allowance (RDA) of 10 mg for children and 15 mg for adults. Not only is milk a good source of dietary zinc it is present in a highly bioavailable form. Milk may also promote the absorption of zinc from other sources such as cereals or vegetables which are themselves rich in phytic acid, a zinc binding substance.

11.8.2.2 Cobalt.   Cobalt is an essential trace element, being present in vitamin B_{12}. Although cobalt levels in milk are low, milk actually supplies about one-quarter of the average dietary contribution.

11.8.2.3 Iodine.   Iodine is an essential element for growth, development and well-being as it is an important component of the thyroid hormones. Iodine deficiency causes enlargement of the thyroid gland in order to compensate for declining production of thyroid hormones.

Iodine deficiency occurs in areas where soils are regularly leached by flooding. The risks are enhanced by presence in the diet of goitrogens which restrict the utilisation of iodine for thyroid hormone synthesis. The absence of dietary selenium enhances the effects of iodine deficiency.

The incidence of goitre—the obvious sign of iodine deficiency—is governed principally by dietary intake and is lower in northern Europe than in central and southern Germany and Italy. These regional differences reflect variation of iodine levels in soils and of fortification of the diet by iodine as, for example, by the use of iodised salt.

Not only is iodine important for humans but it is also important for cattle, hence iodine is regularly given to dairy cattle in the form of feed supplements or mineral licks. The iodine concentration of milk is influenced largely by the cow's dietary intake and to a lesser extent by virtue of residues of iodophor disinfectants or teat dip residues in milk. Because of iodine supplements in dairy cattle diets, iodine in winter produced milk

Table 11.2 Vitamins in milk

Vitamin	Importance	Milk as a source	Percentage contribution of 0.5 litre to reference nutrition intake (RNI)
A (Retinol)	Needed for growth, skin and night vision	Levels depend on cow's diet	40–50
B group			
Thiamin		Milk is a useful	25–30
Riboflavin	Releases energy from food	source of the B vitamin especially B_2 and B_{12}. However,	30–40
Niacin	Release of dietary energy	riboflavin can be destroyed by sunlight	c. 30
Pyridoxin (B_6)	Metabolism of protein required by nervous system.		150
B_{12}	Needed for healthy blood.	B_{12} only found in foods	c.20
Folic acid	DNA & red blood synthesis of animal origin such as meat or milk		c.30
Pantothenic acid	Energy; metabolism		60
Biotin	protein/fat metabolism		100
D	Regulates absorption of calcium; important for growth and maintenance of bones	Milk is a poor source of vitamin D and is sometimes fortified	–
E	Protects PUFA[a] in membranes against oxidation	Low	10–20
K	Needed for synthesis of proteins involved in blood clotting	Present in milk (and most balanced diets)	25
C	Maintains collagen: connective tissue	Milk is a useful source, however, fruit and vegetables are a richer source	15–20

[a]PUFAS—polyunsaturated fatty acids.

is higher than that of summer milk. Milk contains about 70 µg iodine/litre in summer and is five times higher—370 µg/litre—in winter milk.

It is recommended that the average daily iodine intake of adults should be about 140 µg/day. Milk, assuming about 300 ml is consumed per person per day provides about one-fifth of the requirement in summer and one-third of the recommended intake in winter.

The mineral content of milk represents nearly 1% of its weight. The range of elements present is wide and milk makes a major contribution to trace elements essential in man's complex biochemistry. Not only does milk provide many of the trace elements, it offers them in a highly bioavailable form. There are however some deficiencies, notably from iron, copper and manganese, hence infant formula feeds are often supplemented with these trace elements.

11.8.2.4 Bioavailability. There is a variability between humans in their ability to absorb minerals. There is also a great variety of complexity of foods which can affect the absorption of each nutrient (bioavailability). Tannins, for example, which are found in tea, and phytates from cereals, can interfere with iron and other trace metal absorption. It is believed that casein from milk may inhibit the iron-chelating properties of tannins and phytates. Therefore the use of milk in tea and on cereals can improve bioavailability of trace metals not only originating in milk but also from other foodstuffs.

11.9   Vitamins

Vitamins are required in small amounts for the biological function of body cells. Milk is a source of 12 water-soluble and four fat-soluble vitamins. Whilst milk contains all vitamins some are present in small amounts (Table 11.2). Low-fat milks obviously contain less of the fat-soluble vitamins A, D, E and K. Milk is a particularly important source of vitamins B_{12} and B_2 especially for those on vegetarian diets since the only other source of B_{12} is meat.

Further reading

Buttriss, J. (1987) Diet health and the dairy industry. *J. Soc. Dairy Technol.*, **40**(3), 61–64.
Garrett, W.D. (1979) A review of the important trace element in dairy products. *Aus. J. Dairy Technol.*, **3**.
Gunslim, H. *et al.* (1985) Trace elements in human milk, cows milk and infant formalin. *Agric. Biol. Chem.*, **49**(1), 21–26.
Harding, F. (1986) *Dairy Products and their Contribution to the Diet* (Bulletin 48). British Nutrition Foundation, London, pp. 181–185.
Harris, P.G. (1984). Perceived incidence of milk allergy and/or lactose intolerance in Great Britain. *J. Soc. Dairy Technol.*, **35**, 104.
IDF (1983a) *Cultured Dairy Foods in Human Nutrition* (Bulletin 159). IDF, Brussels, Belgium.
IDF (1983b) *Cultured Dairy Products in Human Nutrition* (Document 159). IDF, Brussels, Belgium.
IDF (1983c) *Nutrition and Metabolism* (Document 166). IDF, Brussels, Belgium.
IDF (1984) *Aspects of the Production of Fermented Milks* (Vol. 2, Bulletin 179). IDF, Brussels, Belgium.

IDF (1988) *Milk Products and Health* (Bulletin 222). IDF, Brussels, Belgium.

National Dairy Council, USA (1984). The role of calcium in health. *Dairy Council Digest*, **55**, 1.

Recheigl, M., Jr. *CRC Handbook Series on Nutriton and Food.* CRC Press Inc., USA.

Renner, E. (1989) *Micronutrients in Milk and Milk-Based Products.* Elsevier Applied Science, London, UK.

Renner, E. (1983) *Milk and Dairy Products in Human Nutrition.* Volkwirsha, Pticher Verlag, Munich, Germany.

Robinson, R.K. (ed). (1991) *Therapeutic Properties of Fermented Milks.* Elsevier Applied Science, London, UK.

Shahani, K.M. *et al.* (1979) Nutritional and health aspects of cultured and culture containing dairy foods. *J. Dairy Sci.*, **62**(10) 1685–1694.

Underwood, E.J. (1977) *Trace Elements in Human and Animal Health* (4th edn). Academic Press.

Wong, N.P. *et al.* (1978) Mineral content of dairy products. *J. Am. Dietetic Assoc.*, **72**.

Index